"Stephen Olford has not only spent his life preaching beautiful expository sermons, he is a peerless teacher of preachers. The Stephen F. Olford Biblical Preaching Library provides substantive examples on how to do it. It will be a great help to many preachers."

Dr. R. Kent Hughes, Senior Pastor
College Church, Wheaton, Illinois

"Stephen Olford is a master expositor and genius at outline clarity. . . . Most preachers can neither walk across the street or travel across the continent to hear him. But they can glean the treasures of his preaching life from The Stephen F. Olford Biblical Preaching Library. I heartily commend this resource."

Dr. Maxie E. Dunham, Senior Pastor
Christ United Methodist Church, Memphis, Tennessee

"Every informed preacher of the Word of God knows of the spiritual power, impeccable scholarship, and practicality of the materials produced by Stephen Olford. Without reservation, I commend The Stephen F. Olford Biblical Preaching Library."

Dr. Adrian Rogers, Senior Pastor
Bellevue Baptist Church, Cordova, Tennessee

Books in the Stephen F. Olford
Biblical Preaching Library

The Pulpit and the Christian Calendar 2

Stephen F. Olford

BAKER BOOK HOUSE
Grand Rapids, Michigan 49516

ISBN: 0-8010-6722–7

These resources were adapted from material published by the Institute for
Biblical Preaching, Box 757800, Memphis, TN 38175-7800.

The New King James Version is used as the basis for this Bible study. Also
occasionally used are the King James Version (KJV), the Revised Version (RV),
the New American Standard Bible (NASB), and the New International Version
(NIV).

The author is grateful to the many copyright owners for the use of their
material.

Contents

Introduction

One is a wise preacher, Bible class leader or itinerant evangelist who takes advantage of the Christian calendar of the year for reaching the minds, hearts, and wills of his/her audience. Whether we recognize it or not, the fact remains (even in our secularized society) that people are cuturally conditioned to such seasonal days as Good Friday, Easter, and Christmas.

In this volume we are concentrating on two important seasons of the year. The first is the period that leads up to Good Friday. After an introductory message on "The Word of the Cross" we follow with a thoughtful treatment of our Savior and his suffering for us and our salvation. These seven last words are expositions that will help your listeners to feel that "they were there" when our Lord was crucified. But he rose again!—and that is why we conclude this section with "Journey into Joy."

Then comes Part 2 with Christmas! The focus for this season of the year is Isaiah 9:6. What a text! To paraphrase Dr. Cloason L. Archer, Jr., we have here the character of Immanuel who will bring deliverance to his people. He will be a wonder of a counselor. As mighty God (a term clearly applied to Jehovah in Deut. 10:17; Isa. 10:21; Jer. 32:18), he will be the irresistible battle champion who will achieve the ultimate victory in the arena of history. As everlasting father (lit. father of eternity), he will be not only sovereign of eternity, but source of eternal life to all who believe. As prince of peace, he will bestow shalom. This peace in its fullest meaning suggests health to the sin-sick soul, a sound and saving relation between sinners and God, and a state of righteousness over the earth.[1] What a message for Christmastide and always!

As you stylize these outlines to your own personality as a preacher/teacher, and your own purpose as a pastor, remember what homiletical structure is all about. In the words of Ilion T. Jones: "The outlines should have unity—each point being a subthesis of the main thesis; it should have order, the points being coordinate; it should have proportion, all points being of parallel construction; it should have climax, the points being arranged in an ascending order. The wording should not be odd, smart or clever, but the points should be fresh, striking, and intriguing, without being sensational."[2]

This is precisely what we have sought to do in these expository outlines. So "preach the word! . . . do the work of an evangelist, fulfill your ministry"—and God bless you!

Stephen F. Olford

Part 1

Good Friday and Easter

1

The Word of the Cross
1 Corinthians 1:18–25

"The word of the cross is to them that are perishing foolishness; but unto us which are being saved it is the power
of God" (1:18 RV).

Introduction

The phrase that sums up Paul's concept of the gospel
of our Lord and Savior Jesus Christ is found in verse 18
of this first chapter of 1 Corinthians. It is "the word of the
cross." The phrase is not only expressive but suggestive.
There are three aspects of the word which come to us
from the cross of Christ:

I. The Revelation of God to Men

"The word of the cross is to them that are perishing
foolishness; but unto us which are being saved it is the
power of God" (1:18 RV). The whole idea implicit in this
term "word of the cross" is that of the expression of
thought. It is the word *logos*. And when we ask what is the

nature of this revelation the answer is given us in the context, for example, "Christ the power of God and the wisdom of God" (1:24). In "the word of the cross" we have:

A. The Revelation of the Power of God

"Christ the power of God . . ." (1:24). When God brought creation into being he only had to speak a word, but when he brought redemption to man he had to send the Word. The expression "the power of God" comprehends the total activity of God in Christ by which he made salvation possible for you and me. Consider this in a fivefold way:

1. THE POWER BY WHICH CHRIST CAME

The incarnation of our Lord Jesus Christ was a supernatural act of God. This is clear from the words of the angel to Mary: "The Holy Spirit will come upon you, and the power of the Highest will overshadow you; therefore, also, that Holy One who is to be born will be called the Son of God" (Luke 1:35). Whatever the unbeliever might have to say about the virgin birth it remains a biblical fact that Jesus Christ was supernaturally and sinlessly born into this world.

2. THE POWER BY WHICH CHRIST LIVED

The life of our Lord upon this earth was a supernatural act of God. Paul tells us that "Jesus Christ our Lord . . . was . . . declared to be the Son of God with *power,* according to the Spirit of holiness, by the resurrection from the dead" (Rom. 1:3–4). His sinless life is the greatest phenomenon of the ages. As someone has remarked, "Jesus Christ knew a conscience unclouded by the knowledge of sin."

3. THE POWER BY WHICH CHRIST DIED

The death of Christ was a supernatural act of God, for when Jesus hung upon the cross he was made sin for us, in order "that we might become the righteousness of God in Him" (2 Cor. 5:21). Then having completed his divine mission he voluntarily bowed his head and gave up his spirit. No one ever died like that. This is why Paul says that "the word of the cross is . . . the power of God" (1:18 RV).

4. THE POWER BY WHICH CHRIST ROSE

The resurrection of the Savior was a supernatural act of God. In another place the apostle speaks of the exceeding greatness of God's power, which he wrought in Christ, when he raised him from the dead (Eph. 1:19–20). The miracle of the resurrection includes and supercedes every other miracle which has ever been performed from the beginning of time.

5. THE POWER BY WHICH CHRIST SAVES

The salvation of a sinner through the redemptive work of Christ is a supernatural act of God. This is why Paul exclaims, "I am not ashamed of the gospel of Christ, for it is the power of God to salvation for everyone who believes, for the Jew first and also for the Greek" (Rom. 1:16). At the heart of the gospel is the very dynamic of God which has power to save and to deliver. Nothing in all the universe can transform individuals like the gospel of our Lord Jesus Christ.

Amplification

Show how the rough jailer in Philippi, the runaway slave Onesimus in Rome, and Saul the persecutor on the Damascus road all had the hard core of their resistance broken by the power of the gospel and how their transformed lives bore witness to it before all men.

Illustration

Chundra Lela, an orphaned Hindu girl, made four successive journeys to the cardinal points of India in her

quest for soul-satisfaction. Each involved great personal
suffering. When the weary years of wandering failed, she
entered upon a most severe course of penance, sitting all
day exposed to the burning rays of an Indian sun, sur-
rounded by fires. In the chilly hours of the winter nights,
she half submerged herself in water, all the time wearily
counting the beads upon a chain until the morning sun
appeared over the horizon. Finally, through the simple
words of a gospel message, falling from the lips of a faithful missionary, she was led to believe, and consequently
discarded her idols and every heathen practice in her life.
"Christ crucified" is "the power of God" to save from sin.[1]

B. The Revelation of the Wisdom of God

"Christ the power of God and the wisdom of God"
(1:24). The apostle leaves us in no doubt as to what he
means by "the wisdom of God." A little further down
in this paragraph he says, "But . . . in Christ Jesus . . .
God is made unto us wisdom, and righteousness, and
sanctification, and redemption" (1:30 KJV). The New
American Standard Bible states this even more clearly:
"Christ Jesus, who became to us wisdom from God, and
righteousness and sanctification, and redemption."
Paul is saying that in the wisdom of God we have:

1. THE REVELATION OF CHRIST AS OUR RIGHTEOUSNESS

"Christ Jesus, who became to us . . . righteousness" (1:30 NASB). In and through Jesus Christ we
have been made right, or just, before a holy God.
This aspect of the gospel answers the ancient question, "How then can man be righteous before God?"
(Job 25:4). Because Christ died for our sins and was
raised for our justification (Rom. 4:25), we can know
the righteousness of God imputed to us in response
to simple faith.

Illustration

A group of friends visited an old parish church which
was of great interest. The sexton gave them the key, say-

ing, "You can unlock the door and go in, and I will come shortly." They went to the door, put the key in the lock and tried to open it, but they could not turn the key. They turned and twisted it but to no avail. When they were ready to give up in despair the sexton arrived. "I beg your pardon for giving you so much trouble," he said, "I quite forgot to tell you the door is not locked at all. All you need to do is to just lift the latch and walk in."

Many people are like that group. They try by their own efforts to unlock the door of salvation, but all their efforts are a waste of time. Long ago Jesus Christ unlocked the door, and all we need to do is just to lift the latch and by faith walk in.[2]

2. THE REVELATION OF CHRIST AS OUR SANCTIFICATION

"Christ Jesus, who became to us . . . sanctification" (1:30 NASB). We could never attain holiness in our own strength, but through the indwelling life of Christ the work of sanctification can be accomplished in us day by day. In terms of Christian life and behavior, this means living out *experimentally* what we are *positionally* in Christ, because of his work on the cross.

3. THE REVELATION OF CHRIST AS OUR REDEMPTION

"Christ Jesus, who became to us . . . redemption" (1:30 NASB). The word means "release" or "deliverance." In this particular context it refers not only to the deliverance from the power and penalty of sin, but from the very presence of sin. It is this final act of God by which we are made to conform to the likeness of Christ.

What a revelation is this wisdom of God in the gospel of our Lord Jesus Christ! This revelation is wholly outside of man's capacity to conceive or perceive such a way of salvation, except through the operation of the Holy Spirit. For God has declared that the world by human wisdom cannot know God (1:21).

II. The Proclamation of God to Man

"The word of the cross is to them that are perishing foolishness; but unto us which are being saved it is the power of God" (1:18 RV). God has chosen the foolishness of preaching to communicate the message of the cross. Implicit in this concept of "the *word* of the cross" is not only revelation, but proclamation. Observe that:

A. The Proclamation of the Cross
Is Sometimes Offensive

Paul tells us: "Christ crucified, to the Jews a stumbling block and to the Greeks foolishness" (1:23). In every age religionists and rationalists have found the preaching of the cross to be offensive. To the Jews, it has ever been a stumbling block, and to the Greeks it has always been a laughingstock.

To the religionist, the cross demolishes the idea that he can *work* for his salvation, and this is what makes Calvary so repulsive. There is in man's religious nature that which wants to sacrifice the fruits of his own hands, like Cain of old; or build his own tower of Babel, like the people of Noah's day; or present to God his own filthy righteousnesses, like the scribes and Pharisees of our Lord's time. But the word of the cross destroys such notions and brings us to the hill of Calvary, crying,

> Nothing in my hand I bring,
> Simply to Thy cross I cling.

The rationalist, on the other hand, imagines that he can *reason* his way to God; but God has decreed that man by human philosophy cannot know him (1:21). As the French scientist and philosopher, Blaise Pascal, has ably pointed out, "The supreme achievement of reason is to bring us to see that there is a limit to reason." Nothing pulverizes man's intellectualism quite like the word of the cross. This is why the proclamation of God to man is offensive to those who are perishing.

B. The Proclamation of the Cross Is All Times Decisive

"The preaching of the cross is to them that perish foolishness; but unto us which are saved it is the power of God" (1:18 KJV). The preaching of the cross of Christ is both a drawing power and a dividing power. No one can listen to the gospel message and remain neutral. When the cross is presented in all the simplicity and authority of its message man either rejects it and perishes, or accepts it and lives. This is the unique power inherent in this divine proclamation.

C. The Proclamation of the Cross Is Ofttimes Redemptive

"But to those who are called, both Jews and Greeks, Christ the power of God and the wisdom of God . . ." (1:24). We have already seen that in the wisdom and power of God we have the combined elements necessary for the redemption of man. Thank God, when people hear the call of the gospel and respond they enter into that experience whereby they are saved from the penalty, power, and very presence of sin. This is the glory of the gospel.

III. The Invitation of God to Man

"For the word of the cross is to them that are perishing foolishness; but unto us which are being saved it is the power of God" (1:18 RV). From the cross there shines the light of revelation, proclamation, and invitation. So we have here in this passage:

A. God's Pleasure in the Invitation of the Gospel

"It pleased God by the foolishness of preaching to save them that believe" (1:21 KJV). Paul tells us that

"God's good pleasure" (RV) is that through the foolishness of preaching, men and women should be saved.
Observe that God takes the initiative. The picture is not
of man searching after God, but God seeking man in all
his lostness. Ever since Adam's disobedience cursed the
human race God has been asking, "Where are you?"
(Gen. 3:9).

B. God's Purpose in the Invitation of the Gospel

"The preaching of the cross is to them that perish
foolishness; but unto us which are saved it is the power
of God" (1:18 KJV). Let us remember that every man outside of Christ is lost. Indeed, the verb rendered "perish" (1:18) denotes loss of well-being. A person who is
perishing fails to fulfill the purpose for which God created him. This is where the gospel of Christ meets him
and saves him. The idea behind the word "saved" is
not only that of reclamation but also transformation.

C. God's Process in the Invitation of the Gospel

"It pleased God by the foolishness of preaching to
save them that believe. . . . But unto them which are
called . . . Christ the power of God, and the wisdom of
God (1:21, 24 KJV). Two words sum up the divine process
in the invitation of the gospel. The one is "call," the other
is "believe." The first describes the offer of God; the second denotes the response of man. Jesus is always calling
men and women to himself, and people out of every kin-
dred, tongue, and nation are responding. This process
will continue until the body of Christ is complete.

Illustration

Today we want God's blessings without the pain of
God's purging. We want sermons on how to win friends,
how to have peace of mind, and how to forget our fears.
But we must remember that Christ came to make men
good, rather than merely to make men feel good. Each
Sunday night in my church I give people a chance to come

and pray at the altar. Watching tears streaming down some praying face, I have felt like shouting for joy. The way of the cross is not easy but it is the way home.[3]

Conclusion

The invitation of God to man demands a verdict. If he believes, he is saved; if he rejects, he perishes. As we think of that first Good Friday with all its solemn drama, let us see through the darkness of that mid-day midnight to the eternal light which gleams from that cross. In that light let us see the light of God's revelation, proclamation, and invitation to man; or in the language of our text, "the word of the cross."

The Word of Forgiveness

Luke 23:33–38

"Father, forgive them; for they know not what they do" (23:34 KJV).

Introduction

The last words of a dying friend are always impressive and memorable. Stephen Olford did not have the honor of sitting at the bedside of his father during the closing moments of his dad's life; young Stephen was away conducting an evangelistic crusade. But he was told that his father's last remarks concerning him were, "Tell the lad to preach the Word." These words meant a tremendous lot to him and may explain something of the fire and fervency that inspire his preaching.

Similarly, the words of our Lord, as he hung upon the cross, are precious indeed! We think now particularly of the word of forgiveness–"Father, forgive them; for they know not what they do" (23:34). We marvel as we think of the setting of these words. The Savior was hanging there in agony. Spikes had been hammered through his quivering flesh; the instrument of torture had been raised and allowed to fall into its receptacle with such a jolt that all his bones were out of joint; he had been spat upon; his body had been lacerated with the Roman whips; and in such excruciating pain and agony the first words that fell from his blessed lips were those of forgiveness.

Dr. David Smith in his *Life of Christ* speaks of the kind of thing that often happened when criminals were crucified. They shrieked, yelled, cursed, and spat at their torturers. But here is one who could only say "Father, forgive them" (23:34 KJV). Here we see, first of all:

I. The Prayer of Forgiving Love

"Father, forgive them; for they know not what they do" (23:34 KJV). His first word was a prayer, and in that prayer observe three things:

A. The Submissiveness of His Petition

"Father, forgive" (23:34 KJV). Notice he addresses his Father. Later on we shall be considering another cry that came from his lips: "My God, My God, why have You forsaken Me?" (Matt. 27:46), but here he says "Father, forgive" (23:34 KJV).

A few hours previously he had knelt in the Garden, sweating as it were great drops of blood as he contemplated the meaning of the cross and his identification with sin. There he had prayed, "Father, if this cup cannot pass away from Me unless I drink it, Your will be done" (Matt. 26:42).

Even upon the cross he could have slain these brutal Roman soldiers with a breath from his divine nostrils. But he submitted himself to the will of his Father and became our Savior, that we might know his forgiving love.

B. The Inclusiveness of His Intention

"Father, forgive them" (23:34 KJV). There are those who argue that the "them" refers specifically to the soldiers. But that little word "them" is gloriously inclusive. True, it included those soldiers, but it also included Judas, who went to his own place, not having accepted the forgiveness offered him at the Last Supper. It included Pilate, though it is unlikely that he was ever converted. It included all those priests whose voices were loudest in crying, "Crucify him! Crucify him!" It included every man, woman, and child before and since the cross, for he hung there as the Redeemer and Savior of the whole world.

C. The Redemptiveness of His Contention

"They know not what they do" (23:34 KJV). Did they really *not* know what they were doing? Those soldiers who were familiar with all that was happening in Jerusalem, and knew all about Jesus' preaching must have been challenged again and again as they went to take him and could not, because of the gracious words that proceeded out of his mouth. And surely the priests had some estimation of who he was. Pilate knew, for having weighed the evidence carefully he said, "This Man has done nothing wrong" (23:41 NIV). Even Judas, the son of perdition, knew, for his words were, "I have sinned by betraying innocent blood" (Matt. 27:4). *But such is the forgiveness of God, and the love of our Savior, that he puts the best construction on anything anyone ever does.* "Father, forgive them," he says, "for they know not what they do" (23:34 KJV). Peter expresses the same thought after the day of Pentecost. Addressing the religious leaders he says, "Brethren, I know that you did it in ignorance, as did also your rulers" (Acts 3:17). And the apostle Paul could add: "None of the rulers of this age knew; for had they known, they would not have crucified the Lord of glory" (1 Cor. 2:8). Paul knew something of it in his own heart. As he looked back upon the depths of his sin he had to confess, "I did it ignorantly in unbelief" (1 Tim. 1:13).

Even knowing the fact of sin, however, we cannot fathom the enormity of it. No man will ever live to know the depths of human sin in crucifying Jesus Christ—and we are all included in that act. But such was the redemptiveness of his contention that in love he could say, "Father, forgive them; for they know not what they do" (23:34 KJV).

Illustration

One of the fine novels coming from Sweden in the mid-century was Hemmer's *Fool of Faith*. The setting is Finland during the Communist uprising of 1917. While the revolution succeeded in Russia, in Finland it was repressed, and the prisons were filled with the embittered men who had tried to overthrow the government and the church. The principal character in the story is Pastor Bro, the prison chaplain. The prisoners met him only with hatred and vindictiveness. Failing to reach them, one night in his quarters he prayed for guidance. His prayer took the form of a question, "What would Jesus do if he were the chaplain of this prison?" The answer came, "Jesus would disguise himself as a prisoner, go beyond these gray walls, and minister from the inside." The chaplain did just that, living inside the prison cells and teaching the men about forgiving love. And like Jesus, it cost him his life.[1]

II. The Power of Forgiving Love

"Father, forgive them; for they know not what they do" (23:34 KJV). The ultimate power in the universe is the power of forgiving love. This is what distinguishes Christianity from all other religions and philosophies of men. Within the immediate context of this prayer and in the wider unfolding of biblical truth, we learn of this power of forgiving love.

A. It Is Magnetic

Jesus said, "And I, if I am lifted up from the earth, will draw all peoples to Myself" (John 12:32). The "if" in this verse has the force of "when." There was no doubt in Jesus' mind that he would be crucified, but he implies that "the attraction of the cross would prove to be the mightiest and most sovereign motive ever brought to bear on the human will, and, when wielded by the Holy Spirit as a revelation of the matchless love of God, would involve the most sweeping judicial sentence that can be pronounced upon the world and its prince."[2]

That same redemptive magnetism can vibrate through you and me when Christ and him crucified is magnified through our mortal bodies by life and by lip.

B. It Is Dynamic

"The message of the cross is foolishness to those who are perishing, but to us who are being saved *it is the power of God*" (1 Cor. 1:18). This is precisely what was demonstrated when Jesus cried, "Father, forgive them; for they know not what they do" (23:34 KJV).

The prayers of Jesus are always answered; and we see these answers through the power of forgiving love in human lives. Think of the thief on the cross. He had been hurling abuse at the Savior, as did others standing around the cross. But suddenly he hears this prayer of the Savior: "Father, forgive them; for they know not what they do" (23:34 KJV). He turns, he looks, he believes, and he is saved. "And Jesus said to him, 'Assuredly, I say to you, today you will be with Me in Paradise'" (23:43).

Then there was the centurion standing at the foot of the cross. He was a callous, indifferent, hard-as-nails soldier who ordered his men to do their job and do it quickly. He, too, heard the words of the Lord Jesus and exclaimed, "Certainly this was a righteous Man!" (23:47), or as Matthew has it, "Truly this was the Son of God" (Matt. 27:54).

The power of that forgiving love was also evident at Pentecost, for when Peter stood and preached to that great throng he was speaking to many who had stood at the cross of Jesus. So he said to them, "God has made this Jesus, whom you crucified, both Lord and Christ" (Acts 2:36). Three thousand of them were converted that day, and multitudes afterward, among whom were many priests whose voices had been heard above the clamor of the crowd, crying, "Crucify him!"

And when did Pentecost end? We are still in the period of Pentecost, and that prayer of forgiveness is still being answered today.

Illustration

Forgiving love will not be the active agent in our life as long as we are concerned about our personal rights, or hurts, or injustices. Lloyd Ogilvie writes: "A woman said to me recently, 'Why should I go to her? She hurt me! Let her take the first step.' A man confessed, 'I'm filled with resentment and I'm depressed. I resent people, my job, and what life has dealt me.'" Dr. Ogilvie admonished the man to seek forgiveness where he had been wrong and give forgiveness where necessary. But the man responded, "Why should I do that? I'm the one they should come to." How sad for that man that he did not follow Christ's example, thereby experiencing the power of forgiving love.[3]

III. The Pattern of Forgiving Love

"Father, forgive them; for they know not what they do" (23:34 KJV). This is the pattern of forgiving love for every age and for every Christian. As we forgive others:

A. There Is a Cross That We Must Bear

"Father, forgive them" (23:34 KJV). When Jesus prayed those words he was experiencing excruciating pain. And we do not really forgive until we do it from a heart that is pained and crushed. We cannot show Calvary love without Calvary blood. There is a cross that we must bear if we would be ministers of reconciliation. It costs to be real! It means involvement in the redemptive love of Christ and "the fellowship of His sufferings" (Phil. 3:10).

Illustration

A little boy, being asked what forgiveness is, gave the beautiful answer: "It is the odor that flowers breathe when they are trampled on."

Someone has written:

It is a truth beyond our ken
And yet a truth that all may read:
It is with roses as with men,
The sweetest hearts are those that bleed.
The flower that Bethlehem saw bloom
Out of a heart all full of Grace,
Gave never forth its sweet perfume
Until the cross became its vase.

B. There Is a Christ That We Must Share

"Father, forgive them" (23:34 KJV). I believe Paul has this prayer in mind when he exhorts: "Let all bitterness, wrath, anger, clamor, and evil speaking be put away from you, with all malice. And be kind to one another, tenderhearted, forgiving one another, just as *God in Christ also forgave you*" (Eph. 4:31–32). We have to know the crucified life before we can share the crucified Lord.

Think of three simple illustrations from history. The Book of Acts records the story of Stephen, the martyr, who stood up for his Lord. His only crime was that he preached the gospel. Acts 7 records how his enemies gnashed on him with their teeth and pelted him with stones, and like his Lord before him, he cried with a loud voice, "Lord, do not charge them with this sin" (Acts 7:60). He was paying the price and therefore sharing the gift of forgiveness.

Joseph Robbins was a watchman on a railroad bridge. A neighbor became very jealous of him and wanted to rob him of his money. He waited until payday, and then climbed up onto the bridge with a shotgun. Looking through the window, he saw Joseph Robbins, and took aim and fired. He waited to see if anyone had heard the noise of the shot; then seeing no movement he crashed in through the door. Joseph Robbins was on his knees, and these were his words before he slumped and died, "Holy Father, have mercy on the man that has done this thing, and for Jesus' sake spare him." The man was caught; indeed, he gave himself up, but as he stood in court he said he had been haunted by those words, which had crushed him to repentance.

In 1831 the disease of cholera broke out in Hungary. For some reason or other, the peasant class believed that this was a poison that had been set loose by the nobles, and a revolt started. Tremendous massacres took place, and all manner of excesses. One dear man, who was loved because of his kindness and popularity, was seized by the rebels, dragged through the streets, and beaten repeatedly. In spite of his entreaties, they would not believe him. They took him to a blacksmith's shop and pushed white hot irons into the soles of his feet. The last cry of this dear man of God was like the Master's, "Father, forgive them, for they know not what they do." A miracle happened, for soon those men were running down the street crying, "Have mercy on us! Have mercy on us!"

There we have the pattern of forgiving love in Jesus, in Stephen, in Joseph Robbins, and that Hungarian man of God. So Paul says, "Be kind to one another, tenderhearted, forgiving one another, just as God in Christ also forgave you" (Eph. 4:32).

Conclusion

Forgiveness is the most beautiful word in the Bible because it reflects the most beautiful look in the face of God. It is the word that will inspire the heavenly choirs of the redeemed; for that is what they will sing about: the forgiveness of God (see Rev. 5:9–10). Peter tells us, "Christ also suffered for us, leaving us an example" (1 Peter 2:21). He is the pattern of forgiving love. May we exemplify that power by forgiving others in love.

3

The Word of Assurance
Luke 23:39–43

"Today you will be with Me in Paradise" (23:43).

Introduction

This second "word from the cross" might be called "The Response of the Savior to the Request of the Sinner," and that is how we shall think of it in our meditation now. We can never contemplate the exchanges of that dramatic dialogue without being solemnly impressed with two things: the sinfulness of man, and the sovereignty of God. To crucify the Lord Jesus was the greatest of all crimes, but to add to the shame of it the holy, sinless Son of God was crucified with thieves, brigands, and murderers.

Oh, the exceeding sinfulness and corruption of the human heart! You and I stand there. What happened at Calvary is but the outward expression of all that is inherent in our evil natures. Over against this sinfulness of man, however, is the gracious and wonderful sovereignty of God.

Have you ever pondered why God permitted his Son to be crucified between malefactors? Have you ever realized that all that happened on that fateful day was determined before to be done? Hundreds of years before, Isaiah the prophet foretold that he would be "numbered with the transgressors, . . . and made intercession for the transgressors" (Isa. 53:12). It was an act which magnified the sovereignty and grace of God. Of those two men one became penitent and was gloriously saved—that none need despair, but only one was saved—that none might presume. The impenitent one continued to sleep in his sin, and to all his other transgressions added the impudent irony of railing against the Son of God in his dying moments. One was saved, the other was lost. That is the challenge of the gospel message.

Now let us focus our attention on the dialogue between the Savior and the sinner who was saved. Look, first of all, at:

I. The Sinner's Request

"Lord, remember me when You come into Your kingdom" (23:42). Those words have been preserved for us in the Scriptures because they represent the prayer of men and women for all time who have sought the Savior. They reveal:

A. A Distressing Fate

We read "There were . . . two . . . criminals, led with Him to be put to death" (23:32).

Here was a man whose fate was sealed. Physically, morally, and spiritually, he could do nothing about it. *Physically,* his body was hung up to die. He was there quivering with excruciating pain. He could not lift a hand to work for salvation, not lift a foot to walk in the ways of righteousness. *Morally,* this man had submitted his precious life to the winds of human passion until he had been carried on to the fatal rocks of sin. *Spiritually,* he was "dead in trespasses and sins" (Eph. 2:1). Before he called on the name of the Lord he joined the other thief in reviling the Son of God (Matt. 27:44). So he could not work for his salvation, physically; he could not atone for his salvation, morally; and he could not hope for his salvation, spiritually. He was "without Christ, . . . having no hope and without God in the world" (Eph. 2:12). It was a distressing fate.

B. A Disturbing Fear

"Do you not even fear God, seeing you are under the same condemnation?" (23:40). Here is a man trembling, not only because of the pain pulsating through his frame, but because of a great fear that seized him. It was the fear of:

1. INCRIMINATING DEEDS

"Do you not even fear God," he said to the other malefactor, "seeing you are under the same condemnation? And we indeed justly, for we receive the due reward of our deeds" (23:40–41). In that moment, like John Newton of old, he could see all the sins of his past life flashing before him. He recognized that he would have to answer for every one of them.

Illustration

It is appropriate here to spend a moment on the life of John Newton. When he was 11, his father—a master of a ship in the Mediterranean trade—took the boy on board. Young John was adequately experienced for impressment into the British Navy. Yet John lost his personal discipline, was arrested for desertion, publicly flogged, and demoted to common sailor. While in his teens, John sailed to Africa. He mocked authority, chose his friends unwisely, and became a very unsavory character. In Africa, John fell into the service of a slave dealer, and was put to work on the dealer's plantation, laboring with other slaves. At 21 he escaped, boarded the ship the *Greyhound,* and resumed his former lifestyle. He ridiculed the upright seamen in his company, the ship's captain, and even a book he found on board, *The Imitation of Christ.* One night the *Greyhound* sailed into a violent storm. In the grip of fear, after hours of fighting a losing battle to save the ship, John prayed for the first time in his life. The ship and crew were saved. In gratitude, John Newton became a minister, and we celebrate the change in his life each time we sing, "Amazing Grace! How Sweet the Sound."[1]

The Bible says, "Each of us shall give account of himself to God" (Rom. 14:12). We are in no better position than was the thief on the cross. If we do not know the cleansing power of the blood and know what it is to get right with God, we shall also have to answer for our misdeeds.

2. IMPENDING DOOM

In the light of that he feared he was "under the same condemnation" (23:40). The Scriptures remind us that God hath "appointed a day on which He will judge the world in righteousness by the Man whom He has ordained" (Acts 17:31); and again: "It is appointed for men to die once, but after this the judgment" (Heb. 9:27). One of the things we need to get back to is "the fear of God." If you read Romans 3 you will discover that among the list of things Paul indicates are wrong with men he concludes with these words, "There is no fear of God before their eyes" (v. 18).

Illustration

Dr. Alan Redpath was holding an evangelistic crusade in Belfast, Northern Ireland. After preaching on the subject the judgment of God he left a colleague to conclude the service. Putting a scarf around his neck and pulling a hat down over his eyes, he slipped out one of the exits and stood behind a pillar at the entrance to the auditorium, watching the people as they left the building. As they jostled, jested, and talked, a great lump came into his throat, and his heart pounded. "O God," he prayed, "what is wrong with my preaching? How can a crowd of people come out of a meeting after a message like that and not have the fear of God upon them?"

The Bible says that "the fear of the LORD is the beginning of wisdom" (Prov. 9:10). Where there is no fear there will be no faith. It was only when that earthquake hit the jail at Philippi that the jailer came trembling before Paul and Silas, saying, "Sirs, what must I do to be saved?" (Acts 16:30).

In the sinner's request we see not only a distressing fate and a disturbing fear, but also:

C. A Dawning Faith

"Lord, remember me when You come into Your kingdom" (23:42). What has happened? A moment or two ago he had joined the other thief in mocking the Son of God. What had effected the change? Faith had been begotten in his soul.

This is one of the greatest conversion stories in the whole of the Bible. He did not have the background and privileges that you have, nor the circumstances that characterize this day of grace. He was almost mad with pain, hanging there on that Roman gibbet. Humanly speaking, there was no hope for him whatever. But faith dawned in his soul. Look how it came about:

In the first place, he heard those words of the Savior: "Father, forgive them, for they do not know what they do" (23:34), and he turned his aching head to that middle cross. He saw the words over his head, "THE KING OF THE JEWS" (23:38). Possibly a board hung around the Savior's neck listing the cause for his death—"He called himself the Son of God." Remember, the earthquake had not happened, nor had he uttered the word "Finished!" So it must have been the words of that prayer of forgiveness that brought conviction to his heart, by the Holy Spirit. He paused in his pain to think about it, and faith was born. It was faith in Christ as:

1. THE DIVINE SAVIOR

"Lord, remember me" (23:42). Paul tells us that "no one can say that Jesus is Lord except by the Holy Spirit" (1 Cor. 12:3). Submissive to the workings of the Holy Spirit, this thief stretched out in faith to Christ, the divine Savior. "Think on me," he was praying, "cast an eye my way."

> The dying thief rejoiced to see
> That fountain in his day;
> And there may I, though vile as he,
> Wash all my sins away.
>
> William Cowper

Or think of the chorus:

> I do believe, I will believe,
> that Jesus died for me,
> That on the cross He shed His blood,
> from sin to set me free.

2. THE DIVINE SOVEREIGN

"Remember me when You come into Your kingdom" (23:42). This man's faith has now pierced the heavens. He looks up into the eternal kingdom and sees the arches of that kingdom decorated with the bright garlands from the Tree of Life. He hears the great *Hallelujah Chorus,* as it were, as the angels wait to welcome home the King triumphant, and he cries, "Remember me when You come into Your kingdom" (23:42).

Did you ever hear such faith as this? It is the basis of all salvation: belief in Jesus Christ as Savior and Sovereign. John Calvin says: "How clear was the vision of the eye which could see death in life, ruin in majesty, shame in glory, defeat in victory, slavery in royalty. I question if ever since the world began there has been so bright an example of faith as this."

II. The Savior's Response

"Today you will be with Me in Paradise" (23:43). What a word of assurance is this! What a message to all the children of Adam's race! It gives assurance of:

A. *Immediate Salvation*

"Today you will be with Me in Paradise" (23:43). This is the deathblow to all who tell us that salvation is a matter of working our way by rites and sacraments and good works so as to eventually achieve salvation, or at least the hope of salvation.

"Today," said Jesus. Here is a word which teaches that a crisis, a decision, must take place in the experience of every man and woman, boy and girl, if they are to know salvation. Christ stands and waits for your acceptance, and the moment you call him "Lord," by power of the Holy Spirit, you are saved.

Illustration

Many people have recorded their salvation experience, but none more dramatically shows the immediacy of con version than this one: "The earth slipped a little beneath me as I stood there clutching the edge of the dresser. . . . Ellen didn't smile at all. She was 'listening' to him I knew. I twisted around and fell into the big chair by the window and sobbed, 'Oh God, I wish I were dead!' Ellen didn't come and put her arm around me. . . . Instead she said very calmly and with absolute authority, 'Genie, it would be wonderful if you *would* die! . . . It would be the most wonderful thing that ever happened to you if the old [Eugenia] Price would die right now—this minute, so the new one can be born.' I stopped sobbing, I think. . . . After a few long seconds, Ellen says I looked up at her. The darkness dropped away, and I whispered 'O.K. I guess you're right.' Then Light."[2]

B. Infinite Satisfaction

"Today you will be with Me *in Paradise*" (23:43). I defy anyone to define Paradise. We can talk about it as "heaven," or as the "heavenly Eden," or as the sum and substance of all the joys, bliss, and felicity that we can ever conjure up in the eternity beyond. Whatever it is, it is infinite satisfaction. The psalmist said, "In your presence is fullness of joy; at Your right hand are pleasures forevermore" (Ps. 16:11). And so Jesus says to this wretched robber, brigand, and murderer, "Today you will be with Me in Paradise" (23:43). Salvation is yours.

Illustration

It would be difficult to persuade anyone with that assurance to disbelieve in Christ. This reality was clearly demonstrated in the life of an uneducated factory laborer who radiated the joy of the Lord. One day an unsaved co-worker challenged him to attend a lecture by an atheistic scholar. The believer went to the meeting and listened intently as the speaker launched a logical and forceful attack upon the Christian faith. On the way home, the skeptic asked, "Well, what do you think now?" The answer came quickly, "I heard that lecture 25 years too late." Seeing the puzzled look on the other man's face, he continued, "During the last quarter of a century God has done everything in me and for me that this fellow said was impossible. He's given me peace, answered my prayers, and changed my life."[3]

Conclusion

Is it any wonder that we preach our hearts out in this glorious gospel?

> "Today"—what urgency!
> "With Me"—what company!
> "In Paradise"—what felicity!

Such was the Savior's response to the sinner's request. It is as relevant today as it was two thousand years ago; there is no time dimension with God. Calvary is a point in history, but it is the converging point of two eternities. The cross was in the heart of God long before it was on Mount Calvary. It is a redemptive event for all time and eternity.

Horatius Bonar puts it this way:

> With that shouting multitude,
> I feel that I am one,
> And in that din of voices rude,
> I recognize my own;
> 'Twas I that shed that sacred blood,
> I nailed Him to the tree,
> I crucified the Son of God,
> I joined in mockery.

Will you cry, "Lord, remember me"? If you do, you will hear his voice, "today . . . with Me."

4

The Word of Affection
John 19:25–27

"Jesus . . . said to His mother, 'Woman, behold your son!' Then He said to the disciple, 'Behold your mother!'" (19:26–27).

Introduction

This third word from the cross conjures up one of the tenderest scenes to be witnessed on that all-eventful day. Four women and one man had edged their way up Mount Calvary's slope until they were now standing beneath the center cross. They were Mary, the mother of Jesus; Mary, the wife of Cleophas; Salome, John's mother; Mary Magdalene; and the disciple John. Stunned and silenced by all that had been enacted before their eyes, they stood brokenhearted, helpless, listening. Would the Master speak again? If so, not a word must be missed. We read that "when Jesus therefore saw His mother, and the disciple whom He loved standing by, He said to His mother, 'Woman, behold your son!' Then he said to the disciple, 'Behold, your mother!'" (19:26–27). In that word of affection the Savior lifted all human relationships out of the disharmony and sordidness, into which sin had brought them, into the purity, glory, and wonder of what they can be and mean, through the work of his cross. The relationship featured here is the filial one— the love of a son for his mother. Observe, then, in this word of affection:

I. The Son's Confidence in His Mother

"When Jesus therefore saw His mother" (19:26). That word "saw" carries the thought that he "took in everything." The very sight of Mary would bring back to him the words he had often heard quoted. The saintly Simeon had first uttered them at Jesus' dedication as an eight-day-old infant. Looking at Mary, he had said, "A sword will pierce through your own soul" (Luke 2:35).

True mother love is a costly love, and Mary's was of this quality. No wonder he trusted her. In the first place, here was:

A. A Sacrificing Love

"She brought forth her firstborn Son, . . . and laid Him in a manger" (Luke 2:7). Was ever a mother put in such a plight as Mary? From the moment of conception to the delivery of the child, hers was a sacrificing love. Think of the misunderstanding, misconstructions, and whisperings in her little village. What human being could understand this mystery? Yet she carried it bravely.

Think again of that tender scene in the stable with lowing cattle and bleating sheep, where she brought forth her firstborn Son, wrapped him in swaddling clothes, and laid him in a manger. Did ever a mother sacrifice like that?

B. A Sheltering Love

"Behold, an angel of the Lord appeared to Joseph in a dream, saying, 'Arise, take the young Child and His mother, flee to Egypt, and stay there until I bring you word; for Herod will seek the young Child to destroy Him'" (Matt. 2:13). Away there in Egypt, cut off from home and loved ones, Mary sheltered that little life from those who were seeking to destroy him. Then they came back to Nazareth, and we see something of:

C. A Succoring Love

"He [Jesus] went down with them and came to Nazareth, and was subject to them" (Luke 2:51). Mary was bringing up the little lad with all the tender care and thoughtfulness of a mother who truly loved. It could not have been long after that that Joseph died. This is not stated in Scripture, but the very silence concerning him, supported by history, seems to indicate that he died when Jesus was but a boy.

Hers was also:

D. A Submitting Love

Remember the story of John 2. In a moment of crisis at the wedding in Cana of Galilee, Mary had come to Jesus saying, "They have no wine." And he replied, "Woman, what does your concern have to do with Me? My hour has not yet come" (John 2:3–4). At first glance these words may suggest a measure of rebuke. Very likely, Mary may have been expecting Jesus to use this predicament as a means of calling attention to himself in a way that would have furthered his messianic mission, but his *hour* had not yet come. Without disputing the matter, Mary showed her submissiveness to the authority of her Son, now the anointed Servant. She stood back and waited, knowing that he could and would do something.

Later, at Calvary's cross, hers was:

E. A Suffering Love

"There stood by the cross of Jesus His mother" (19:25). Those who love most deeply suffer most intensely.

Illustration

A woman was calling on a friend whose children were brought in. The caller said, evidently with no thought of the meaning of her words, "Oh, I'd give my life to have two such children," to which the mother replied with subdued earnestness, "That's exactly what it costs."[1]

Can you imagine what this brave, heartbroken, yet controlled woman suffered while she stood at the base of that cross? "There He hung before her eyes," says Stalker, "but she was helpless. His wounds bled, but she dare not staunch them; His mouth was parched, but she could not moisten it; . . . The thorns round His brow were a circle of flame around her heart."

It was in the knowledge of all this that "Jesus . . . saw His mother" (19:26).

II. The Son's Courtesy to His Mother

"Jesus . . . saw His mother, and . . . said . . . 'Woman'" (19:26). The highest possible courtesy is embodied in this term "Woman," or "Lady." The Lord Jesus fulfilled to the letter that ancient command, "Honor your father and your mother" (Exod. 20:12). Three times in the Gospels he addresses his mother, and in each case there is a courtesy which breathes obedience, honor, and respect.

In the first instance, there is:

A. The Courtesy of an Approved Son

"Why is it that you sought Me? Did you not know that I must be about My Father's business?" (Luke 2:49). At the age of twelve, when he became "a son of the law," Joseph and Mary had taken Jesus up to Jerusalem for the Feast of the Passover. When it was over and they were on their way home, Jesus, unknown to them, lingered behind. After a three-day search they found him in the temple, sitting among the doctors of the law, asking questions and answering with such understanding that they marveled. "Why is it that you sought Me?" he asked his mother, "Did you not know that I must be about My Father's business? . . . Then He went down with them and came to Nazareth, and was subject to them. . . . And Jesus increased in wisdom and stature, and in favor with God and men" (Luke 2:49–52).

In the next instance we see in him:

B. The Courtesy of an Anointed Servant

"Woman, what does your concern have to do with Me? My hour has not yet come" (John 2:4).

Jesus was now 30 years of age which, according to the Old Testament, was the age of responsibility. As he stood on the banks of the Jordan, the heavens opened, the Spirit of God descended as a dove and rested upon him, and a voice declared, "This is My beloved Son, in whom I am well pleased" (Matt. 3:17). No doubt Mary was there, and she would understand what this meant. He was no longer the little "Jesus boy," but God's anointed servant.

So it was that later, at the wedding at Cana of Galilee, when she knew that there was a shortage of wine, she came to him with confidence and put the situation before him. Then Jesus said, "Lady, leave it to me," and she went away and told the servants to be ready to do whatever he told them.

Illustration

Many of the world's greatest leaders have bowed in submission to their mothers. For example, Balzac, giant of French letters, continued to sign his letters to his mother,

"Thy obedient son." Even though his influence and repu-
tation as an author grew beyond bounds, his devotion to
his mother was evident in those three words, "Thy obedient son."[2]

C. The Courtesy of an Appointed Savior

"'Woman, behold your son!' Then He said to the disciple, 'Behold your mother!'" (John 19:26–27). Who can
tell the suffering through which Mary passed, as she
stood by the cross and looked at that bespittled face,
with blood trickling down from his thorn-crowned
brow, and his wounded hands and feet. She knew that
he was indeed the Savior of the world. It was in the
midst of such agony that he looked down and said,
"Lady, there is your son!" and to his disciple, "John,
behold your mother!" Oh, the courtesy and thoughtfulness!

Surely, this is a word to young people and, indeed,
to all here. Have you courtesy for your parents? You
can never be disobedient, dishonoring, or discourteous
again when you have stood by that cross.

III. The Son's Care of His Mother

"When Jesus therefore saw His mother . . . He said . . .
'Woman, behold your son!' . . . 'Behold your mother!'"
(19:26–27). Here is an example for all whose parents are
still living. In these callous and materialistic days there is
a growing disregard on the part of young people for their
parents. Remember the words of St. Paul: "If any widow
has children or grandchildren, let them first learn to show
piety at home and to repay their parents; for this is good
and acceptable before God. . . . But if anyone does not
provide for his own, and especially for those of his house-
hold, he has denied the faith and is worse than an unbeliever" (1 Tim. 5:4, 8). Notice, first of all:

A. The Selflessness of the Son's Care of His Mother

"When Jesus . . . saw . . ." (19:26). Suffering can be selfish: for people can draw attention to themselves through it, to evoke pity and help. But not so with Jesus. All his words thus far were for others. There he was, walking along the Via Dolorosa, bleeding from head and back, bowed down with the weight of that cross. As the women wailed and lamented, he turned to them and said, "Daughters of Jerusalem, do not weep for Me, but weep for yourselves and for your children" (Luke 23:28). His thought was for them.

Then later, his prayer for those who crucified him on a Roman gibbett was, "Father, forgive them, for they do not know what they do" (Luke 23:34). And to the repentant thief who hung at his side, his words were, "Today, you will be with Me in Paradise" (Luke 23:43).

Now once again he opens his mouth in concern for his mother. Not only was there the selflessness, but:

B. The Thoughtfulness of the Son's Care of His Mother

"Woman, behold your son!" (19:26). Who was he referring to? Not the brothers of his family, for they did not believe on him until after Pentecost. There was only one person with whom he would leave his mother, and that was John. He had proved himself because of *his love.* He had found his way right to the bosom of the master and, as no other, had entered into the significance of his teaching. Then there was *his loyalty.* John was the first disciple to turn back and stand at the cross. Notice *his liberality.* His was a favored home—one in which Mary would be well cared for. Jesus wanted the best for her.

Illustration

That same tone of concern is seen in the account of a gentleman in a large city whose practice it was to spend a few minutes each evening with his mother. His mother lived three blocks distant, and for thirty years her son had never failed to go and bid her goodnight, if he was in the city. "No matter what the weather may be, no matter who his guests are, my husband never fails to run over to his mother's and bid her goodnight," said the gentleman's wife. "When his business compels him to be away from the city, he writes to her every day, if only a single line. Her mental powers are beginning to fail, and she forgets many things, so that her mind is blank on some points; but when nine o'clock comes she always knows the hour, and says, 'It is time for Henry to come and bid me good-night.'"[3]

C. The Costliness of the Son's Care of His Mother

"Woman, behold . . ." (19:26). Observe that Jesus did not call Mary "Mother"—even on this last occasion. He was breaking the painful truth that henceforth there would not be the son/mother relationship.

The first time he had called her "Woman," or "Lady," there was the transition from an approved Son to an anointed Servant. Now there was the transition from an anointed Servant to an appointed Savior. Never again could she say "Son." Never again could he say "Mother." From that moment onward he was moving into another realm. No one could rival his media-torial ministry, no one woman could have prominence in his life—even his mother. Mary Magdalene, who would caress his feet, must not touch him until he had gone to heaven and represented his love dispassion-ately for the entire world. So Mary looked at Jesus for the last time in a natural union. After Pentecost there would be a mystical union, and she would be just a humble disciple.

Conclusion

The cross is where human relationships are *sanctified* and also *surrendered,* for there does come a time—perhaps when one is called to the mission field—when this has to take place. In an infinite sense, it happened at Calvary; in a relative sense, as one is called to cut relationships for the master. But it is at the cross that relationships are finally *satisfied.* In the last analysis, Mary would not have had it any other way. Only when our relationships converge at the cross are they sanctified, surrendered, and truly satisfied.

5

The Word of Anguish

Matthew 27:33–50;
2 Corinthians 5:17–21

"My God, My God, why have You forsaken Me?" (Matt. 27:46).

Introduction

We stand once again at the foot of the cross. It is now midday. For three hours the suffering body of Jesus has been exposed to the burning rays of the sun. His tortured mind has been subjected to the taunts of a ribald crowd and the assaults of the merciless powers of evil. The divine sufferer has almost reached the point of exhaustion when a supernatural phenomenon takes place. The sun is at its zenith, yet darkness falls over the whole earth. Such a darkness could not have been due to an eclipse, for it was at the time of full moon. It is a darkness that can be felt. We can imagine people returning to the city, wailing with fright, as they beat their breasts and say to one another, "Surely the judgment of God is about to fall upon

47

us!" Suddenly a cry is heard through that midday midnight—the cry of the Son of God—"My God, My God, why have You forsaken Me?" (Matt. 27:46).

Martin Luther once sat for hours (some believe days) without food, or even disturbing his posture, gazing at those words. Then at last he rose, with amazement written all over his face, and he cried from the depths of his soul: "God forsaken of God, who can explain that?" And he never wrote anything on that text.

So with chastened spirits and subdued hearts, let us allow these words to burn into our souls and to stir us to a new love and surrender to the one who gave himself for us. Consider, first of all, how this cry of anguish expresses:

I. The Faithfulness of the Son of God

"My God, My God . . ." (Matt. 27:46). Something is happening there in the darkness which will never be comprehended by finite minds in time or eternity.

> . . . none of the ransomed ever knew
> How deep were the waters crossed,
> Nor how dark was the night that the
>   Lord passed through,
> Ere He found His sheep that was lost. . . .
>
>   Elizabeth Clephane

In the midst of the darkness God is dealing with his Son in a way that passes human comprehension. Here is:

A. The Faithfulness of His Reciprocal Love

He would recall his own words: "Therefore My Father loves Me, because I lay down My life that I may take it again" (John 10:17), and he uses that term of personal affection, "*My* God, *My* God." His reciprocal love is unshaken and unshakable, even though God had to hide his face from him.

B. The Faithfulness of His Responsive Trust

"My God, My God . . ." (Matt. 27:46). The word *Eloi* means "the strength of God," as if to say, "O my God, I must trust thee in the midst of anguish, agony, and darkness." How like the words of Job before him: "Though He slay me, yet will I trust Him" (Job 13:15). Had the faithfulness of the Son of God broken down, the substitutionary character of his death would have been invalidated. But with all the physical suffering at the hands of men, the mental suffering at the hands of Satan, and the spiritual suffering at the hand of God, he was unshakable in his love and trust.

Illustration

Fanny Crosby, blinded as an infant by faulty medical treatment, wrote some 8,000 hymns; she could write "All the Way My Savior Leads Me" because she saw God's hand at work in her hardship. In her autobiography, Crosby spoke of that erring physician and the overruling care of her Great Physician: "But I have not for a moment, in more than eighty-five years, felt a spark of resentment against him because I have always believed from my youth to this very moment that the Good Lord, in His Infinite Mercy, by this means consecrated me to do the work I am still permitted to do."[1]

II. The Forsakenness of the Son of God

"My God, My God, why have *You* forsaken Me?" (Matt. 27:46). "I can understand the nation forsaking me," he might have said, "for they never recognized in me the Messiah." "He came to His own, and His own did not receive Him" (John 1:11). Again, "I can understand my own family forsaking me," for "even His brothers did not believe in Him" (John 7:5). I can understand even my disciples forsaking me, for "all the disciples [had forsaken] . . . Him and fled" (Matt. 26:56). "But O My God, why have *You* forsaken Me?" It is hard to understand the meaning

of that word "forsaken," but in its true etymological con-
notation it means "dereliction," "separation," or "leaving
entirely alone."

Why did God hide his face from him and leave him
entirely alone? There is only one answer: because of *sin*.
In Psalm 22 where these words are quoted—"My God, My
God, why have You forsaken Me?" (v. 1)—we find they
are followed by the words, "But You are holy, who
inhabit the praises of Israel" (v. 3). In that moment the
Lord Jesus was identifying himself with:

A. The Reality of Sin

Paul tells us: "He made Him who knew no sin to be
sin for us, that we might become the righteousness of
God in Him" (2 Cor. 5:21). He did not merely take upon
him guilt, but sin in all its ugly reality. Our feeble
minds reel at the thought of it. Imagine the purest character you have ever known being brought into the most
loathsome surroundings. Cause that body to be brought
into contact with all the disease, corruption, and loath-
someness of sin in its outworking; and bring upon
that spirit and soul the sense of guiltiness and culpa-
bility and awfulness of sin and you begin to understand
what it meant for Jesus to be "made sin." David fore-
shadowed Christ in the messianic Psalm that cries, "My
God, My God, why have You forsaken Me? . . . I am a
worm, and no man" (Ps. 22:1, 6). The word for "worm"
there is *cocus.* It is the little worm that was crushed to
produce the red dye for the coverings of the tabernacle
and for the robes of the high priest. From it were
extracted the crimson and scarlet, which symbolized
sin in its essence. John 3:14 says: "As Moses lifted up
the serpent in the wilderness even so must the Son of
Man be lifted up." Why was the serpent lifted up in the
wilderness? It was a symbol of the very thing that was
slaying the camp of Israel. The venom and poison of
the snake were represented in that brazen serpent. So

the Lord Jesus was identified with the reality of sin; and also with:

B. The Totality of Sin

"All we like sheep have gone astray; we have turned, every one, to his own way; and the LORD has laid on Him the iniquity of us *all*" (Isa. 53:6). John the Baptist, pointing to Jesus said, "Behold! The Lamb of God who takes away the sin of the world!" (John 1:29). God focused on him the sin of the whole world. We cannot imagine what that could mean. As a magnifying glass focuses the rays of the sun upon one point so that it immediately burns with concentrated heat, so the misery, crime, pollution, corruption, and guilt of all the human race, in its most concentrated form, was made to focus upon the head of the Son of God.

He was identified not only with the reality and totality of sin, but with:

C. The Fatality of Sin

"The soul who sins shall die" (Ezek. 18:4); and again: "The wages of sin is death" (Rom. 6:23). It was not merely physical death which was sealed with those words, "It is finished!" (John 19:30), it was hell—alienation from God. In those three hours a whole eternity of hell was compressed into the experience of our Savior.

When two friends love each other dearly, the longer their friendship is unbroken, the more tragic and painful it is when the breach comes. Can you imagine, then, how terrible it must have been, in the experience of our Lord Jesus Christ, who had never known one moment of unbroken fellowship with his Father, to have him hide his face from him? No wonder we hear his cry of dereliction.

Praise God, however, there is a light which gleams from that darkness. In the word of anguish we have:

III. The Fulfillment of the Son of God

"My God, My God, why have You forsaken Me?" (Matt. 27:46). During those hours of separation and unspeakable anguish not a word passed from the lips of the Savior. But now he has emerged, the sun is about to break through again, and as he looks back on that shattering experience he says, "Why have You forsaken Me?" (Matt. 27:46). It was a completed act. He is about to make it official to a world of angels and principalities. The reverberations of the shout—"It is finished!" (John 19:30)—are being felt all over the world until this present hour. There was a fulfillment of all the love, grace, and mercy of God in Christ for men and women like you and me. He was forsaken that we might never be forsaken. "God was in Christ reconciling the world to Himself, not imputing their trespasses to them" (2 Cor. 5:19). When the Savior was made "to be sin" for us (2 Cor. 5:21), the whole work of reconciliation was completed so that we might be:

A. Reinstated

"God was in Christ reconciling the world to Himself, not imputing their trespasses to them" (2 Cor. 5:19). We are now made to appear before God in a favorable light, as if we had never sinned. What matchless grace and unbounded love for a loathsome sinner! God "devises means, so that His banished ones are not expelled from Him" (2 Sam. 14:14). Because we have been clothed in his righteousness we can now sit down under his shadow "with great delight" (Song of Sol. 2:3).

Illustration

Over the years a terrible barrier had grown between Sara and her father, Marc. She had been abused as a child and later, as an adult, had harbored bitterness and anger toward her father. But now with God as her heavenly Father all of that was gone. As Sara explained to Marc what had happened to her, tears flooded his eyes. Quickly she rose from her chair to kneel beside him. She reached for his hand, "Oh, Pop! I love you! I've had resentment toward you for the way you treated me. I resented being shut out. I resented being the scapegoat of this family. But today those feelings left me . . . as if they were erased. I've been set free. God has forgiven me . . . and because I'm forgiven I'm free to love you! . . . I forgive you, Pop, for all the hurts you've given to me. I love you . . . I want this to be a new day for us. Just accept my love. It's real." Clumsily he returned her embrace, then kissed her. There was no need for words.

B. Re-created

"If anyone is in Christ, he is a new creation; old things have passed away; behold, all things have become new" (2 Cor. 5:17). Praise God, we can know what it is to be not only clothed in righteousness, but created in righteousness, and so be "partakers of the divine nature." (2 Peter 1:4). Paul writes in Romans 8:15—"You received the Spirit of adoption by whom we cry out, 'Abba, Father.'"

Illustration

Everett Fullam in his book, *Living the Lord's Prayer,* records this experience: "It was mid-July in 1969, and I was more than a hundred miles into the interior of Liberia. The place was so remote that the residents had not even heard the name Africa, let alone America. . . . Yet it was there in that raw, backward section of the small West African nation that I had one of my most memorable experiences, driving home to me what it means to know God as Father. The moment came when I was invited to baptize three converts from paganism—people who had come to know the love of the Father through the grace of Jesus Christ, although they . . . knew little about science and the universe. There were two men and one woman. We stood on the banks of a muddy river, wet and happy. I had never seen three more joyful people. "What is the best thing about this experience?" I asked. All three continued to smile, the glistening water emphasizing the brightness of their dark-skinned faces but only one spoke in clear, deliberate English: "Behind this universe stands one God, not a great number of warring spirits, as we had believed, but one God. And that God loves me."[2]

Conclusion

Have you heard the confession of the faithfulness of the Son of God? Have you listened to the expression of his forsakenness? Have you appreciated something of the impression of his fulfillment? There can be only one reply to this word of anguish of the Savior and that is to gladly surrender our lives for his service; or in the words of T. L. Hargrave:

> Oh, matchless grace, that Jesus there alone
> On Calv'ry's cross for sinners should atone:
> To such a Friend, a Savior and a King,
> Our lives for service we will gladly bring.

The Word of Agony
John 19:28–30; Psalm 69

"Jesus . . . said, 'I thirst!'" (John 19:28).

Introduction

Jesus has already hung some six hours on the cross. The blood vessels of his sacred body are almost dried up. A dreadful fever rages through his frame. His tongue is parched and cleaves to his jaw. His lips are swollen and burn like fire. The spiritual desolation through which he has just passed has practically exhausted any remaining strength.

"Will he ever speak again?" we ask. "Can anyone so tortured by pain formulate intelligible words?" Yes, wonder of wonders, he speaks again! "I thirst," he says. It is the word of agony, for there is scarcely a greater torment known to man than that of insatiable thirst. Travelers who have experienced it in the burning deserts of the East fill us with horror as they describe the bleeding mouths, bulging eyes, hoarse cries, and unutterable agony of the thirst of death. This was our Savior's lot when he said, "I thirst." With reverent minds and chastened spirits let us consider how this word of agony reveals:

I. The Reality of the Savior's Humanity

"After this, Jesus . . . said, 'I thirst!'" (John 19:28). "This word," says D. M. Panton, "strikes a deathblow at the denial of the real humanity of Christ. Angels do not thirst, a phantom or an apparition does not thirst; it is the *man* Christ Jesus who thirsts."

A. He Thirsted in Life

"Jesus . . . being wearied from His journey, sat thus by the well. It was about the sixth hour. A woman of Samaria came to draw water. Jesus said to her, 'Give Me a drink'" (John 4:6–7).

Dr. J. Oswald Sanders once said, "God does not thirst, but the Man Christ Jesus did thirst, for He was 'God manifest in the flesh'" (1 Tim. 3:16). While not ceasing to be all that he was essentially before the Incarnation, he so readily partook of our humanity that the sinless infirmities common to man became his. "In all things He had to be made like His brethren, that He might be a merciful and faithful High Priest" (Heb. 2:17).

B. He Thirsted in Death

"Jesus . . . said, 'I thirst!'" (John 19:28). He opened his ministry with a gnawing hunger (Matt. 4:2); he closed it with an agonizing thirst (John 19:28). It was the same Jesus, the one who sat by the well. He had undergone no change.

"Thirst is a commonplace misery," says C. H. Spurgeon, "such as may happen to peasants or beggars; it is no royal grief; therefore, Jesus is Brother to the poorest." The Savior, however, endured thirst to an extreme degree, for it was the thirst of death; and even more than this, the thirst of one whose death was for every man.

Illustration

A medical doctor provides some of the physical descriptions of what it is like to be crucified—especially in relation to thirst. He writes: "As the arms fatigue, cramps sweep through the muscles, knotting them in deep, relentless throbbing pain. With these cramps comes the inability to push [oneself] upward to breathe. Air can be drawn into the lungs but not exhaled. He fights to raise himself in order to get even one small breath. Finally carbon dioxide builds up in the lungs and in the blood stream, and the cramps partially subside. Spasmodically he is able to push himself upward to exhale and bring in life-giving oxygen.

"Hours of this limitless pain, cycles of twisting, joint-rending cramps, intermittent partial asphyxiation, searing pain as tissue is torn from his lacerated back as he moves up and down against the rough timber. Then another agony begins: a deep, crushing pain deep in the chest as the pericardium slowly fills with serum and begins to compress the heart.

"It is now almost over—the loss of tissue fluids has reached a critical level—the compressed heart is struggling to pump heavy, thick, sluggish blood into the tissues—the tortured lungs are making a frantic effort to gasp in small gulps of air. The markedly dehydrated tissues send their flood of stimuli to the brain. Jesus gasps . . . 'I thirst.'"[1]

Sufferers throughout the ages have derived comfort from the fact that they "do not have a High Priest who cannot sympathize with our weaknesses, but was in all points tempted as we are, yet without sin" (Heb. 4:15). Isaiah reminds us, "In all their affliction He was afflicted" (Isa. 63:9). So as we hear that word from the cross—"I thirst"—we are assured that there is:

. . . No throb nor throe,
That our hearts can know,
But He feels it above . . .

                    W. E. Littlewood

Illustration

Arriving at Chester, England at 2 A.M. on a cold winter's night, after a rough passage across the Irish Channel, Dr. A. T. Schofield found he had several hours to wait for the train to his final destination. The station was cold, desolate, and terribly drafty, being open from end to end. In the waiting room he found a porter, sweeping out the room. Engaging him in conversation, he learned that the man had worked nights for many years, though plagued with rheumatism. Still his face wore a happy patient look. Curious to know, and half suspecting the old porter's source of comfort, Schofield said that there was not much comfort in being frozen to death with cold. The man's face lit up as he replied, "Oh! sir, it is not that, but what I was thinking of before you came in—what love it was of Jesus to go and take a body that could feel, and go through all his sorrow and suffering down here that he might be able to understand all my cold and pain this night, while he's up there in heaven. I know his feeling for me. He knows and understands all I suffer; and when I think of him feeling for me up there I don't half mind the pain. Oh! 'tis a wonderful thing—his love—isn't it, sir?" Needless to say, the time flew by as both men talked of the Good Shepherd's love and care.

II. The Extremity of the Savior's Humiliation

"Jesus . . . said, 'I thirst!'" (John 19:28). There was:

A. The Humiliation of the Creator's Thirst

"Jesus . . . said, 'I thirst!'" (John 19:28). Remember that even though he was "the Man Christ Jesus" (1 Tim. 2:5) he never for one moment ceased to be "Creator of the rolling spheres, ineffably sublime!" He it was who scooped out the ocean beds, arranged the setting of the lakes, planned the trickling brooks, ordered the course of the mighty rivers, and initiated the system of the rainfall. All the resources of the universe were at his disposal, even as he hung upon that cross. And yet the Creator stopped to ask aid from one of his executioners. "I thirst," he said. Oh, the unspeakable humiliation of the Creator's thirst!

B. The Humiliation of the Redeemer's Thirst

"Jesus . . . said, 'I thirst!'" (John 19:28). It was not long since the Savior had cried, "My God, My God, why have You forsaken Me?" (Matt. 27:46). Into that moment of time had been compressed such a torment of hell as would be experienced by the whole human race. That torment of hell was the agonizing thirst of lost souls.

During his ministry, Jesus depicted the thirst of one lost soul in hell. He described him as "being in torments . . . and . . . [seeing] Abraham afar off, and Lazarus in his bosom. Then he cried and said, 'Father Abraham, have mercy on me, and send Lazarus that he may dip the tip of his finger in water and cool my tongue; for I am tormented in this flame'" (Luke 16:23–24).

This, then, was the utmost humiliation of Jesus in order that he might become your Redeemer and mine. The Scripture that was going through his tortured mind, and being fulfilled in that hour of his extreme humiliation and agony, was undoubtedly Psalm 69: "I am weary with my crying; my throat is dry; my eyes fail while I wait for my God. . . . Draw near to my soul, and redeem it; deliver me because of my enemies. You know my *reproach,* my *shame,* and my *dishonor;* . . . Reproach has broken my heart, and I am full of heaviness; I looked for someone to take pity, but there was none; . . . They also gave me gall for my food, and for my thirst they gave me vinegar to drink" (vv. 3, 18–21). Truly, having "humbled Himself [He] . . . became obedient to the point of death, even the death of the cross" (Phil. 2:8).

III. The Avidity of the Savior's Hopefulness

"Jesus, knowing that all things were now accomplished, that the Scripture might be fulfilled, said, 'I thirst!'" (John 19:28). No one can read these words without discerning the unshakable confidence and hopefulness of the divine Sufferer. He had thirsted throughout his whole Calvary experience, but it is now that he gives expression to thirst. The night of sinbearing is over. It only remains for him to cry with a loud voice, "It is finished!" (John 19:30). Why thirst now? Surely, in addition to what we have already considered, it was the thirst for:

A. The Father's Commendation of His Redemptive Work

Just before the cross he prayed, "'Father, glorify Your name.'" and there was a voice from heaven, saying, "I have both glorified it and will glorify it again" (John 12:28).

At the beginning of his ministry, as he stood on the banks of the Jordan, the heavens were opened and a voice said, "This is My beloved Son, in whom I am well pleased" (Matt. 3:17). The Father had been well satisfied with his Son's hidden life. Then, again, at the zenith of his ministry, having demonstrated his full qualifications to become our Redeemer, the heavens were opened and the Father once more declared his pleasure in his beloved son.

But now, as he hangs on the cross, he thirsts. He has experienced what we cannot possibly understand: the awfulness of being forsaken of God. As he became our sinbearer, an eternity of fellowship was broken, and he longed for the restoration of his Father's smile and the commendation of his redeeming work. For this "joy that was set before Him [He] endured the cross" (Heb. 12:2).

That thirst included also the hope of:

B. The Sinner's Recognition of His Redemptive Work

When Jesus said to the woman of Samaria, "Give Me a drink" (John 4:7), there was more than a physical thirst in that request. Jesus had meat to eat and drink, too, that even his disciples did not know of. It was the carrying out of his Father's will. There was a primary sense in which he wanted a drink, and he asked it of the woman as a point of contact; but behind that request was also a deep longing, a thirst, for love, obedience, and devotion. That thirst reached its utmost hopefulness when on the cross he said, "I thirst" (John 19:28).

Illustration

Two men that were characterized by a redemptive passion were Dr. J. H. Jowett and General William Booth. Dr. Jowett once said that "the gospel of a broken heart begins with the ministry of bleeding hearts"; and again: "As soon as we cease to bleed, we cease to bless." General Booth added that he would like to send all his candidates for officership to hell for twenty-four hours, as the chief part of their training. Only thus would they be able to accept the sacrifice of winning the lost.[2]

In the light of all that has been brought before us, have you satisfied his thirst? Has the Lord Jesus seen the travail of his soul and been satisfied in you?

Read the account of the soldier who took a sponge, dipped it in vinegar, and pressed it to the lips of the Savior. Undoubtedly, there was compassion in that mockery. Even from a cruel, indifferent, hardened Roman soldier there was some response, some touch of pity. Peter wasn't there, John wasn't there, and even the women were not there to respond to that dying request.

Perhaps, when we get to glory, we can ask the Lord what happened to that man!

Conclusion

Jesus is thirsting still. What have you given him to drink? Is it the sour wine of pity and mockery, or is it the sweet wine of unreserved love, devotion, and full surrender? Only as we satisfy his heart will we know the satisfaction of our own hearts. This is what David means when he says, "Delight yourself also in the LORD, and He shall give you the desires of your heart" (Ps. 37:4). And Jesus said, "Blessed are those who hunger and thirst for righteousness, for they shall be [satisfied]" (Matt. 5:6).

The Word of Triumph
John 19:28–30

"It is finished!" (19:30).

Introduction

The sun which has been shrouded in darkness for three hours shines again, as if to announce the dawn of a new day. Abraham, with all the Old Testament saints, rejoiced to see this day, and was glad (see John 8:56). And those who have lived since the cross look back to it as the most significant and important day in the history of the world.

From the moistened lips of Jesus, who has been treated to a sip of vinegar administered on hyssop, comes the *greatest* word of triumph. Matthew tells us that he cried with a loud voice (see Matt. 27:46). John records what he said—"It is finished!" (John 19:30), or more literally, "Finished," or "Accomplished." "This," says J. Oswald Sanders, "is the greatest single word ever uttered." And J. Flavel adds, "Here is a sea of matter in a drop of language." We shall spend eternity contemplating this shout of victory. Meanwhile, there are four thoughts that suggest themselves to us. In this cry of triumph we have:

I. The Word of Completion

"It is finished!" (19:30). With what relief, as well as release, the Savior cried, "It is finished!" (19:30). For him, this word of completion indicated:

A. The Fulfilled Word of God

"After this, Jesus, knowing that all things were now accomplished . . . said, . . . 'It is finished!'" (19:28, 30). All that Scripture had said concerning him in relation to his birth, life, and death—whether in promise, picture, poetry, or prophecy—had now been fulfilled. After his resurrection, the master had to upbraid his disciples for not appreciating this fact. He said to them, "These are the words which I spoke to you while I was still with you, that all things must be fulfilled which were written in the Law of Moses and the Prophets and the Psalms concerning Me. . . . Thus it is written, and thus it was necessary for the Christ to suffer and to rise from the dead the third day" (Luke 24:44, 46).

B. The Finished Work of God

"Jesus, knowing that all things were now accomplished" (19:28). During his ministry he had spoken more than once about finishing the work which the Father had given him to do. Think of the occasion at the well of Sychar where he said, "My food is to do the will of Him who sent Me, and to finish His work" (John 4:34). Later, he declared, "I have a greater witness than John's; for the works which the Father has given Me to finish—the very works that I do—bear witness of Me, that the Father has sent Me" (John 5:36). When he offered the sublime high-priestly petition for himself and the disciples he prayed, "I have glorified You on the earth. I have finished the work which You have given Me to do" (John 17:4).

Now the great task of the ages—the redemption of a lost world—had been fully accomplished. Every obstacle between man and God had been removed, every demand of the law satisfied, and the sin question fully dealt with. All the types and shadows of the old covenant had been fulfilled in him (see Heb. 10:11–12). The work of God which he came to do was complete.

Amplification

Compare this triumphant word with Cecil Rhodes' cry of frustration, as he lay on his deathbed, "So much to do, so little done!" For Christ there were no regrets. He could shout, "It is finished!" (19:30).

II. The Word of Conquest

"It is finished!" (19:30). Says J. Oswald Sanders: "The previous two words from the cross express its tragedy; this saying proclaims its triumph. The word of dereliction changed to a cry of jubilation." This was no cry of a victim, but the shout of a victor. This word of conquest announced the Savior's:

A. *Triumph over the World*

Anticipating this moment on Calvary's cross, Jesus said, "In the world you will have tribulation; but be of good cheer, I have overcome the world" (John 16:33).

The apostle John defines the world as "the lust of the flesh, the lust of the eyes, and the pride of life" (1 John 2:16); in other words, the evil system of life which is opposed to the Father. It is that in the world which depraves human appetites—"the lust of the flesh"; that which debases human esthetics—"the lust of the eyes"; that which degrades human ambitions—"the pride of life." James states categorically that "friendship with the

world is enmity with God" (James 4:4); but in the cross
of Christ the world has been overcome (see Gal. 6:14).

B. Triumph over the Flesh

The Roman epistle declares: "What the law could
not do in that it was weak through the flesh, God did
by sending His own Son in the likeness of sinful flesh";
and again: "Our old man was crucified with Him
[Christ], that the body of sin might be done away with,
that we should no longer be slaves of sin" (Rom. 8:3;
6:6).

To quote Dr. Joseph Macaulay: "The flesh is the
devil's beachhead and the world's camping-ground in
the heart of the believer. It is not the whole man, but
that self which demands the service and obedience of
the whole man."

Thank God, when Jesus cried, "It is finished!" (19:30),
he overcame the flesh for every sinner who truly
believes. So the apostle Paul testifies: "I have been crucified with Christ; it is no longer I who live, but Christ
lives in me; and the life which I now live in the flesh I
live by faith in the Son of God, who loved me and gave
Himself for me" (Gal. 2:20).

C. Triumph over the Devil

As the shadow of the cross fell across his path, Jesus
declared, "Now is the judgment of this world; now the
ruler of this world will be cast out" (John 12:31). Then
came the cross with its mighty conflict. Never did the
devil fight harder, but never was he more convincingly
defeated. We read that "Having disarmed principalities
and powers, He made a public spectacle of them, tri-
umphing over them" (Col. 2:15); and again we read that
"through death He [destroyed] . . . him who had the
power of death, that is, the devil" (Heb. 2:14). In virtue
of this mighty conquest, James exhorts us to submit to
God and resist the devil (see James 4:7). Since Jesus has
conquered the world, the flesh, and the devil, sin

should not have dominion over us (see Rom. 6:14). Indeed, we can be "more than conquerors through Him who loved us" (Rom. 8:37). Hallelujah! for the shout of triumph, "It is finished!" (19:30).

Illustration

Years ago, African slaves had huge iron collars placed around their necks to which were attached binding chains. This prevented them from escaping, though it often bruised their tender throats and cut off respiration. When freedom came, the best part was being loosed from their chains and those confining iron bands. Are you bound by Satan? Does he have your neck in the iron stocks? There is only one who can release you from the fearful collar of condemnation, and that is Jesus. As Charles Wesley wrote:

> He breaks the power of canceled sin,
> He sets the prisoner free;
> His blood can make the foulest clean;
> His blood availed for me.

III. The Word of Consecration

"It is finished!" (19:30). The Greek word for "finished" is the same as that which is translated "consecration," or "dedication." Speaking of Christ, the writer to the Hebrews says, "the Son, who is consecrated for evermore" (Heb. 7:28 KJV). The question arises as to when this consecration was completed or perfected, and the answer is when he cried, "It is finished!" (19:30). That moment on the cross marked:

A. The Perfection of the Obedience of Christ

"Though He was a Son, yet He learned obedience by the things which He suffered. And having been perfected, He became the author of eternal salvation to all who obey Him" (Heb. 5:8–9). One of the tests of true consecration is the life of obedience. Although the Lord Jesus had no propensity to evil or rebellion, yet he had to demonstrate that, as a son, he could learn obedience. So Paul writes that "being found in appearance as a man, He humbled Himself and became obedient to the point of death, even the death of the cross" (Phil. 2:8). Peter adds, ". . . Christ also suffered for us, leaving us an example, that you should follow His steps" (1 Peter 2:21). If he had to learn obedience, how much more you and me.

B. The Perfection of the Offering of Christ

"Christ, who through the eternal Spirit offered Himself without spot to God . . ." (Heb. 9:14). The sacrifice which Jesus made was without blemish and without spot; it was both worthy and wholehearted. In the light of such consecration Paul says: "I beseech you therefore, brethren, by the mercies of God, that you present your bodies a living sacrifice, holy, acceptable to God, which is your reasonable service" (Rom. 12:1). No wonder C. T. Studd exclaimed, "If Jesus Christ be God, and died for me, then no sacrifice is too great for me to make for Him."

Illustration

When John McNeill, the Scottish evangelist, landed in France during the war, he was introduced to the general in command, who said he would like to give him suggestions about his preaching to the men. The general wanted McNeill to tell the men that if they died it would be all right for them in the next world, since they had died for their country. The evangelist's reply was, "General, if one of the men under your command were to be awarded the Victoria Cross for valor, and I were to belittle the deed by which the decoration was won, you would not like it. And I want to tell you, General, that you are cheapening my Lord's sacrifice." The incident ended at that point.[1]

IV. The Word of Challenge

"It is finished!" (19:30). Leslie F. Church says: "This word of triumph was not spoken into the empty air. Beyond the sigh of relief, beyond even the report of the Son to the Father, was the proclamation to men." No one can hear this greatest word that has ever been spoken since the beginning of the world without being profoundly challenged. Let us consider, in closing, the significance of this word of triumph. In the word of *completion* we have the challenge of:

A. The Believer's Certainty in Christ

"It is finished!" (19:30). This word of completion *secures the believer's justification*—"being justified freely by His grace through the redemption that is in Christ Jesus, whom God set forth to be a propitiation by His blood, through faith" (Rom. 3:24–25). It also *procures the believer's sanctification* "through the offering of the body of Jesus Christ once for all" (Heb. 10:10). What is more, it *ensures the believer's glorification*—"whom He justified, these He also glorified. . . . He who did not spare His own Son, but delivered Him up for us all, how shall He not with Him also freely give us all things?" (Rom. 8:30, 32). On the grounds of the finished work of Christ, the believing sinner can know what it is to be justified, sanctified, and glorified. Someone has written:

> 'Tis finished! here our souls can rest,
> His work can never fail;
> By Him, our Sacrifice and Priest,
> We enter in the Veil.

In the word of *conquest* we have the challenge of:

B. The Believer's Victory in Christ

"It is finished!" (19:30). Every believer can share in that note of triumph (see 2 Cor. 2:14). In the train of that triumph we are assured of victory over the world, the flesh, and the devil. Ours is not to fight *for* victory but *from* victory, and we can know what it is to be "more than conquerors through him who loved us" (Rom. 8:37).

In the word of *conquest* we have the challenge of:

C. The Believer's Ministry in Christ

"It is finished!" (19:30). Our privilege is to begin where he finished. "He died for all, that those who live should live no longer for themselves, but for Him who died for them and rose again. . . . Now all things are of God, who has reconciled us to Himself through Jesus Christ, and has given us the ministry of reconciliation. . . . Therefore we are ambassadors for Christ" (2 Cor. 5:15, 18, 20). In response to such self-giving love, we cannot do less than consecrate our lives to the ministry of *living* for Christ and *preaching* for Christ.

Illustration

Hudson Taylor was interviewing some young people who had volunteered for the Lord's service. He asked several practical questions to find out how well qualified they were for the life they were anticipating. The answers were varied. "I want to reach others across the sea because Christ has commanded us to go into all the world and preach the gospel to every creature," one replied. Another said, "I want to go because millions are dying without ever having heard of Jesus, the only One who can save them." Others had similar answers. Hudson Taylor looked at them thoughtfully for a moment and then said, "All of your motives are good, but I fear they will fail you in times of severe testing and tribulation—especially if you are confronted with the possibility of having to face death for your testimony. The only motive that will enable you to remain true is stated in 2 Corinthians 5:14. *Christ's love constraining* you will keep you faithful in every situation."[2]

Here, then, we have *the ministry of consecrated living* (see 2 Cor. 5:15) which demands the dethronement of self and the enthronement of Christ. It was with the cross before him that Jesus said to his disciples: "If anyone desires to come after Me, let him deny himself, and take up his cross, and follow Me" (Matt. 16:24). For the Lord Jesus, this consecration was consummated on the cross and meant an obedience and an offering of perfection. We, too, must carry our cross until we can say, "It is finished!"

The ministry of consecrated preaching calls for the ministry of reconciliation (see 2 Cor. 5:15, 18, 20), together with the method of an ambassador. If we know anything of victory in Christ we will want to share this message and plead with others to be reconciled to God.

Conclusion

We have seen the implications and interpretations of this word of triumph heard from Calvary's cross. Let us see that this word spells out for us completion, conquest, consecration, and challenge. Only then will our lives be so lived that we shall be able to say, "I have fought a good fight, I have *finished my course,* I have kept the faith" (2 Tim. 4:7 KJV).

The Word of Confidence
Luke 23:46–49

"Father, into Your hands I commend My spirit" (23:46).

Introduction

We now come to the last word of the seven spoken from the cross. As we examine this final utterance we find that it is mainly concerned with the divine sonship of our Lord.

When brought before Caiaphas and asked whether he was the Christ, the Son of God, Jesus answered, "It is as you said. Nevertheless, I say to you, hereafter you will see the Son of Man sitting at the right hand of the Power, and coming on the clouds of heaven. Then the high priest tore his clothes, saying, 'He has spoken blasphemy!'" (Matt. 26:64–65). And when Pilate declared, "I find no fault in Him," the mob cried out, "We have a law, and according to our law He ought to die, because He made Himself the Son of God" (John 19:6–7).

So in this word from the cross we hear Jesus affirming his sonship and saying, "Father." If Jesus Christ is not the Son of God, then there is no revelation of the love of God. Were we to read John 3:16 like this—"God so loved the world that he gave an archangel," it would have no appeal. It would be like a millionaire tossing a coin to a beggar in the street—costing him nothing. But when we read that "God so loved the world that He gave His only begotten Son" we are melted and moved.

Unless we believe in the doctrine of the divine and eternal sonship, we cannot believe in Christ's atonement for sin, for only one who is infinite can pay the ransom price for the human race. No created or finite being is equal to the total act of God's creation. He must be the uncreated one—co-equal, co-eternal with the Father. If we do not believe in the divine sonship, then we know nothing of the message of a divine saviorhood—"the Father . . . sent the Son as Savior of the world" (1 John 4:14).

So we see the significance of the words, "Father, into Your hands I commend My spirit" (23:46). His Calvary experience commenced with a prayer for others, "Father, forgive them, for they do not know what they do" (23:34). It concluded with a prayer, this time for himself—"Father, into Your hands I commend My spirit" (23:46). Here, then, is affirmed:

I. Christ's Confidence in the Security of His Sonship

Hanging on the cross, Jesus could say, "Father, into Your hands I commend My spirit" (23:46). Throughout his life he had confidence in the security of his sonship. At the age of 12 he said to his earthly parents, "Did you not know that I must be about My Father's business?" (Luke 2:49). Again and again throughout the gospels he referred to that filial relationship, and as he bows his head to die he breathes the word "Father."

Illustration

> A devoted father came into the room where his eight-year-old was dying of an incurable disease. The child, sensing that he was not going to get well, asked his father, "Daddy, am I going to die?" "Why, son, are you afraid to die?" The child looked up into the eyes of his father and replied, "Not if God is like you, Daddy!"[1]

In considering the security of his sonship, it is important that we see in the Savior's final prayer:

A. The Revelation of the Essence of Sonship

When Jesus uttered the words, "Father, into Your hands I commend My spirit" (23:46), he was giving expression to one of the cardinal doctrines of the Christian faith. Canon Liddon, of St. Paul's in London (1870–90), says: "The words 'only begotten' mean not merely that God has no other Son; but that His only begotten Son is, by virtue of this sonship, a partaker of the incommunicable and imperishable essence which is sundered from all created life by an impassable chasm." When Jesus said "Father," he was claiming co-equality and co-eternity in the one divine essence. He had ever been "Son," and he still was "Son." Although he had gone through hell and had cried the cry of dereliction, he could still say "Father."

B. The Restoration of the Enjoyment of Sonship

As the Savior prayed, "Father, into Your hands I commend My spirit" (23:46), he announced the restoration of the enjoyment of sonship. You see, when Jesus died on Calvary's tree, the Father had to turn his face from him. What that meant to the son of God you and I will never know. We shall never be able to fathom the depths of that cry of dereliction—"My God, My God, why have You forsaken Me?" (Matt. 27:46). The *relationship* between the Father and the Son remained the same; but the fellowship had been broken. That, to our precious Lord, was an eternal truth compressed into three hours. But now the darkness was passed, the shout of victory had reverberated in the air for *fellowship* had been restored.

This is a parable and a doctrine all in one, and we can know this last word of the cross in terms of personal experience. When we came to know Christ as personal Savior and Lord, we were born into the family of God. The Bible says, "As many as received Him, to them He gave the right to become children of God, even to those who believe in His name" (John 1:12). Once we are in God's family we know a relationship that nothing in hell, on earth, or in heaven can ever sever. However, we also recognize that every time sin invades our lives fellowship is broken, and it is only when we claim forgiveness and cleansing, by virtue of the cross, that sin is pardoned and we can look up into God's face once again and say "Father."

But there is another aspect of truth which is implicit in this last word of the cross. It is:

II. Christ's Confidence in the Dependency of His Sonship

We can sense this dependency as we read those words, "Father, into Your hands I commend My spirit" (23:46). Just as he manifested confidence in the *security* of his sonship throughout his life and in the hour of death, so he also demonstrated confidence in the *dependency* of his sonship.

A. *In Life He Was Completely Dependent upon His Father*

We have reason to believe that every morning he prayed Psalm 31:5, from which this last word of the cross is undoubtedly quoted. It is the prayer that every godly Jewish mother taught her baby as soon as syllables could be formed. The verse reads, "Into Your hands I commit my spirit; You have redeemed me" Jesus put the word "Father" before it and deleted the phrase, "You have redeemed me," since it did not apply to him. His prayer every day was "Father, into Your hands I commend My spirit" (23:46). That was the attitude of his life. In his *words* he never spoke without dependency on his Father. He could declare, "The words that I speak to you I do not speak on My own authority; but the Father who dwells in Me" (John 14:10). Concerning his *works,* he could say, "I can of Myself do nothing. . . . I do not seek My own will but the will of the Father who sent Me. . . . the Father who dwells in Me does the works" (John 5:30; 14:10).

Go through the gospels and observe how this relationship of dependency worked out in all areas of his ministry. Consider *his teaching ministry.* In Matthew 11 we find him teaching his disciples, and in this context he lifts his eyes to heaven and prays, "I thank You, Father, Lord of heaven and earth, because You have hidden these things from the wise and prudent and have revealed them to babes. Even so, Father, for so it seemed good in Your sight" (vv. 25–26). It is quite evident that he could not adequately minister to his disciples without dependency upon his Father.

Consider *his healing ministry.* We see Jesus in the region of Decapolis. A man who was deaf and had a speech impediment was brought to him to be healed. The Savior touched him and lifted his eyes to heaven in prayer. Then he turned to the man and said, "Be opened," and we read that the man's ears were unstopped and his tongue released, so that all who stood by were amazed (Mark 7:34–37).

Then we watch him standing by the grave of his beloved friend Lazarus. Before he calls forth a man who had been dead for four days he demonstrates his dependency upon his Father, once again, by looking up to heaven and praying, "Father, I thank You that You have heard Me. And I know that You always hear Me, but because of the people who are standing by I said this, that they may believe that You sent Me" [in other words, that all power comes from heaven through the Father-Son relationship]. Then "He cried with a loud voice, 'Lazarus, come forth!' And he who had died came out" (John 11:41–44).

Consider *his feeding ministry.* When he took the loaves and the fishes to break and feed the multitudes he first of all looked into his Father's face and said, "I thank Thee." Such was the dependency of the Son of God throughout his life.

Illustration

At the 1951 session of the Southern Baptist Convention in San Francisco, M. T. Rankin led a prayer of thanksgiving for the life of martyred missionary William Wallace. The prayer included this sentence, rich in illustrative value, "God is too wise to make a mistake, too good to do evil." That's the confidence that Jesus had in his Father.[2]

B. In Death He Was Completely Dependent upon His Father

When the moment for death had come he could say with simple confidence, "Father, into Your hands I commend My spirit" (23:46).

In Psalm 16 we find words that were obviously in his mind as he anticipated the dismissal of his spirit. He could say, "I have set the Lord always before me; because he is at my right hand I shall not be moved. Therefore my heart is glad, and my glory rejoices; my flesh also will rest in hope. For You will not leave my soul in Sheol, nor will You allow Your Holy One to see corruption" (Ps. 16:8–10). You will observe that in this text the totality of his being is mentioned. In the act of dependency Jesus was virtually saying, "Father, concerning my body, I trust you to see that it will not suffer corruption. Father, concerning my soul, I trust you not to leave it in Hades. Father, concerning my spirit, I commend it to you here and now."

What a comforting word this should be to all true believers in our Lord Jesus Christ! No wonder the apostle Paul exhorts the saints in Thessalonica not to "sorrow as others who have no hope" (1 Thess. 4:13). Even in the hour of death we can know with absolute confidence that the body, soul, and spirit are taken care of.

Illustration

There is a lovely story told by George MacDonald of a mother who had two sailor boys. She had often been taunted by infidel neighbors concerning the precarious life they were living. "You will lose them; they will drown like so many other sailor boys," they would say. "But they will still be safe," the mother would reply. "What do you mean safe, if they are drowned?" "Have you never read what is under the sea?" the old lady explained, as she quoted Isaiah 40:12—"'Who [holdeth] . . . the waters in the hollow of his hand.' If they drown, they'll fall right into His hands."

III. Christ's Confidence in the Authority of His Sonship

When Jesus prayed, "Into Your hands I commend My spirit" (23:46), he was exercising his rightful authority as the Son of God. We can illustrate this in two significant ways:

A. On Calvary's Cross Jesus Ordered Death

In the words "Father, into Your hands I commend My spirit" (23:46), he was gathering up all that was involved in the method, manner and moment of his death.

As to the *method,* he had told his disciples already that "the Son of Man must be delivered into the hands of sinful men, and be crucified, and the third day rise again" (Luke 24:7). On a number of occasions his enemies had attempted to put him to death by stoning, lynching, or throwing him over a precipice, but his hour had not yet come. Jesus knew by what method he would die, and nothing could change that.

As to the *manner* of his death, the Savior was just as confident. We are told that when death approaches, the dying are overcome with weakness and then there is the final gasp before the physical frame collapses; but this was not so with our Lord. The Bible tells us that he *bowed* his head (John 19:30). That word "bowed" is the same as that which is used in Matthew 8:20 where Jesus declares that "the Son of Man has nowhere to lay His head." Just as deliberately as he would lay his head in sleep, so our wonderful Savior positioned his head in strength and confidence when he prayed, "Father, into Your hands I commend My spirit" (23:46).

As to the *moment,* our wonderful Lord was just as clear and certain. To us, death is always the master, but to him death was his servant. Indeed, when the moment arrived, he dismissed his spirit with absolute precision and poise. He is the only one who has ever done this. St. Augustine put it perfectly when he wrote: "He gave up His life because He willed it, when He willed it, and as He willed it."

Illustration

Only rarely does one hear of a voluntary substitutionary death, but there is one story that comes to mind which occurred during World War II. Because a prisoner had escaped from Auschwitz, the inmates of Block 14A were lined up by the Germans. Sgt. Franciszek Gajowniczek of the Polish Army was chosen for death as a reprisal. Overcome, he cried out, "My poor wife, my poor children. Goodbye." At that moment, prisoner No. 16670, Father Maximilian Kolbe, stepped forward, approaching the camp's deputy commander. "I would like to die in the

place of the man who has the wife and children." The substitutionary death of Father Kolbe allowed Gajowniczek to
live.[3]

B. On Calvary's Cross Jesus Overcame Death

This is the pledge implicit in the words "into Your
hands I commend My spirit" (23:46). He deposited his
spirit in order to take it again when the moment of resurrection arrived. The words of that prayer were the
earnest of his triumph over the grave. He had already
declared "Therefore My Father loves Me, because I lay
down My life that I may take it again. No one takes it
from Me, but I lay it down of Myself. I have power to
lay it down, and I have power to take it again. This
command I have received from My Father" (John
10:17–18).

So as he hung upon that cross in those closing
moments of his redeeming work he could look through
the gloom into the glory, through death into life,
through apparent tragedy into absolute victory. In the
language of Psalm 16 again he could exclaim, "You will
show me the path of life; in Your presence is fullness
of joy; at Your right hand are pleasures forevermore"
(v. 11).

Conclusion

In this word of the cross, then, we see Christ's confidence in the security, dependency, and authority of his
sonship. May we likewise have such confidence, day by
day, as we commit spirit, soul, and body into the Father's
hands. May we ever live in the center of his will, walking
in the pathway of his choice, serving in the interests of
his work—in life, and even in death.

Journey into Joy
Luke 24:13–35

"Two of them were traveling that same day to a village called Emmaus, which was about seven miles from Jerusalem. . . . While they conversed and reasoned, . . . Jesus Himself drew near and went with them" (24:13, 15).

Introduction

The Holy Spirit has recorded this immortal story in order to teach us many lessons; supremely, that everyone of us is on the journey of life. Matthew does not record this story, nor does Mark or John, but Luke includes it in his Gospel because there is something very human about it.

The two disciples in question (some commentators believe they were husband and wife) were not part of the apostolic band. They had turned their backs on Jerusalem, with its tragedy of the cross, and were facing the sinking sun as they walked westward to Emmaus, about seven miles away.

In this account of their journey, we see the whole purpose of God, in the glorious message of the gospel, tenderly, truthfully, and thrillingly told. Notice three things about this journey into joy:

I. The Divine Conversation

"And they talked together of all these things which had happened. . . . While they conversed . . . Jesus Himself drew near and went with them" (24:14–15).

Ever since Creation, man has been on a journey. God saw how sad and slow of heart men were on that journey, as a result of sin entering the world, and so he sent his blessed Son to converse with men, for "Jesus Christ is God's conversation with men." Just as Jesus drew near and went with those two disciples on that first Easter morning, so he has joined men and women ever since on the journey of life. John says in his prologue: "In the beginning was the Word, and the Word was with God, and the Word was God. . . . And the Word became flesh and dwelt among us [came alongside of us on the journey of life]" (John 1:1, 14).

In his walk with these two, the Lord Jesus noticed two things about them that are true of us—unless we know the wonder and joy of the resurrection message.

A. He Found Sad Hearts

"Jesus Himself drew near and went with them. . . . And He said to them, 'What kind of conversation is this that you have with one another as you walk and are sad?'" (24:15, 17).

Are you joyful? Is there happiness in your heart, or are you part of the vast throng walking the journey of life who are sad because they have never invited the Lord Jesus into heart and home?

These two were sad because their faith was shaken. Later in their conversation they said, "Are You the only stranger in Jerusalem, and have You not known the things which happened there in these days?" (24:18).

They believed, as others did, that the one who had entered Jerusalem on that Palm Sunday, riding on a steed, would redeem Israel. They believed that he would drive out the Romans and establish the great messianic kingdom—but it had not materialized. Instead, he had been crucified—stabbed to death with nails in his hands and feet—and their faith was gone.

All over the world, at this hour, there are people whose faith has been shaken. Religion has failed. As far as they are concerned, all that they hoped that the church would accomplish has failed. They have looked to certain Christian leaders, who have not measured up to expectation, and so their faith has been sadly shaken.

Furthermore, these two were sad because their hope was shattered. They had enough religious knowledge to know the meaning of three days. The disciples had also heard this prophet, who was "mighty in deed and word" (24:19), say that in three days the temple of his body would be raised up; but three days had gone by and nothing had happened.

Their faith was shaken, their hope was shattered, but what is more, their love was stifled. These disciples had loved this prophet. They had seen him perform miracles, they had seen him touch the heads of little children, they had watched him break bread and fish to feed the multitudes, they had seen him raise the dead, and heal the leper—but now he was gone.

Nothing is more frustrating than stifled love—when somehow you cannot love him anymore: He's gone, he's buried, he's lost. The Lord Jesus communed with them; and, today, Jesus himself draws near, sent by his Father in heaven to join you on life's journey, to discuss your shaken faith, the dreams that have been unfulfilled, the love which is unsatisfied.

B. He Found Slow Hearts

"He said to them, 'O foolish ones [O simple ones, O shallow ones], and slow of heart to believe in all that the prophets have spoken!'" (24:25). The reason the Lord Jesus Christ came into this world was to expose the reason for your sadness and slowness of heart; the reason why you cannot penetrate the deep things of God; why the whole of Scripture seems inexplicable; why prayer is a farce, and the church a puzzle; why God seems so unreal and far away. Remember, you are a religious being and you carry the similitude of God in your personality, even though you have been cursed by sin.

This couple did not understand what transpired on that rugged cross. They did not understand the meaning of that outpoured blood. They did not understand that the stone rolled away from the tomb was one of the greatest miracles the world had ever seen.

Jesus Christ never meets anyone along life's journey without starting a conversation. He has to speak, he has to expose the slowness and unbelief of hearts. He has also come to renew us with his resurrection life.

II. The Divine Confrontation

"'Ought not the Christ to have suffered these things and to enter into His glory?' And beginning at Moses and all the Prophets, He expounded to them in all the Scriptures the things concerning Himself" (24:26–27). God sent his Son into this world not only to initiate a conversation with men, but to eventuate a confrontation with men. He came in order that he might talk to us in our language and expose, by what he said, the emptiness and unbelief of our hearts. The Lord Jesus Christ confronts us with:

A. Prophetic Truth·

"'O foolish ones, and slow of heart to believe in all that the prophets have spoken! Ought not the Christ to have suffered these things and to enter into His glory?' And beginning at Moses and all the Prophets, He expounded to them in all the Scriptures the things concerning Himself" (24:25–27).

Beginning at Moses, he showed that he was the fulfillment of God's Law (that was the patriarchs); he showed that he was the fulfillment of God's life (that was the psalmist); he showed that he was the fulfillment of God's love (that was the prophets). He was the fulfillment of "all the Scriptures" (24:27). What an impact! What a confrontation!

B. Historic Truth

"'Ought not the Christ to have suffered these things and to enter into His glory?'" (24:26). Addressing the very event of which they were speaking, he showed that he was the historic fulfillment of what he said would happen. Prophecy had become history. Their problem was their failure to accept what was taught in Bible prophecy. As Leon Morris points out: "The prophets had spoken plainly enough, but the minds of Cleopas and his friend had not been quick enough to grasp what was meant. The word *all* [that the prophets had spoken] is . . . important. They had no doubt seized on the prediction of the glory of the Messiah, but it was quite another thing to take to heart the prophecies that pointed to the darker side of His mission. . . . the passion was not simply a possibility that might or might not become actual, depending on the circumstances: it was *necessary*. Written in the prophets as it was, it had to happen."[1]

C. Dynamic Truth

"And they said to one another, 'Did not our heart burn within us while He talked with us on the road, and while He opened the Scriptures to us?'" (24:32). Even as he talked with them we read that their hearts began to burn within them.

If you are prepared to recognize the presence of the Lord Jesus on life's journey you will discover that conversation will turn to confrontation because no one can encounter the Lord Jesus and be the same again. He alone can change the sadness of heart into gladness of heart.

That confrontation with the living Lord made them do something. Having reached Emmaus, he indicated that he would go on, but they constrained him to abide with them, seeing it was evening, "and he went in to stay with them" (24:29). The Lord Jesus never forces himself upon anyone. The Savior will not enter your life without an invitation; you must ask him to come in.

Illustration

Thomas Bilney, an Englishman who died a martyr's death in 1531, describes how he came to know the Lord. He says, "My soul was sick and I longed for peace, but nowhere could I find it. . . . But at last I heard of Jesus Christ. It was then, when first the New Testament was set forth by Erasmus, that the light came. I bought the book, being drawn by the Latin rather than by the Word of God, for at that time I knew not what 'the Word of God' meant. On my first reading I chanced upon these words, 'This is a faithful saying, and worthy of all acceptance, that Christ Jesus came into the world to save sinners, of whom I am chief.' This one sentence through God's inward working did so light up my poor bruised spirit that the very bones within me leaped for joy and gladness. It was as if, after a long dark night, day had suddenly broke." God can do the same for you![2]

III. The Divine Consummation

"And He went in to stay with them. Now it came to pass, as He sat at the table with them, that He took bread, blessed and broke it, and gave it to them" (24:29–30). The most wonderful thing about any journey is that it reaches its consummation. Notice what that consummation meant to those two individuals:

A. He Satisfied Their Hearts

"Did not our heart burn within us while He talked with us on the road, and while He opened the Scriptures to us?" (24:32).

The Lord Jesus always starts at the center, then moves out to the circumference. Think of the conversion of John Wesley. During his student days this Oxford-trained man visited the jails and prisons around Oxford out of compassion for people He tried to preach the gospel but found that he had no power in his life. He left Britain and came to the United States and started to preach in the state of Georgia, but discovered he had no message. Sadly disillusioned, he returned to England by ship. During a storm he saw some Moravian Christians so alive with God that they could look death in the face unafraid. On arrival in the U.K., he searched out a Moravian brother and asked how he could know what it meant to be justified by faith. Intellectually, he was convinced that a man could be justified by faith but, experientially, it did not mean anything until that 24th of May, in Aldersgate, when in a company of simple believers a Christian layman read aloud the preface to Martin Luther's Commentary on Romans. As he listened, "his heart was strangely warmed." From that moment he became the revivalist that shook a nation for God and eventually saved Britain from a revolution of blood.

Has your heart been strangely warmed? Can you say, "My heart burns within me?" The consummation of any journey into joy must start with a warmed heart

B. He Sanctified Their Home

"It came to pass, as He sat at the table with them, that he took bread, blessed and broke it, and gave it to them" (24:30). He turned their home into a sanctuary, and the meal into a sacrament. That is what Jesus does every time he comes into your "house-life"; he makes it a sanctuary.

But he also turned the meal into a sacrament. He took the bread and broke it, and in the way he broke that bread they must have seen the marks in his hands, and their eyes were opened. They knew him; and he vanished from their sight, so that they did not need to see him anymore. He had entered their heart, their home, and that bread had become a sacrament. Isn't it wonderful to think that every meal can be a sacrament, a little communion service?

Illustration

Some missionaries in China visited a couple in their humble abode, after they had newly accepted the Lord Jesus as their Savior. The couple had cast out all their gods and were eager for more instruction in the way of righteousness. The missionaries were hungry as they sat down before a low table on which were placed two dishes. One contained some squash boiled in water; the other had the poorest kind of rice—all they could afford. Beside it was a rock of black salt, such as is given to cattle in the United States, but which served as their table salt. The host dipped it into the dish of squash to season it. The missionary expected to be asked to give thanks for the food, but instead Mr. Ch'eng stood up, looked upward to the soot-begrimed ceiling, and prayed very reverently, "Please heavenly Father, partake with us!" The missionaries were touched at this act of courtesy toward God. His presence was very real in that home.[3]

C. He Sealed Their Happiness

"So they rose up that very hour and returned to Jerusalem, and found the eleven and those who were with them gathered together, saying, 'The Lord is risen indeed'" (24:33–34). Scholars have pointed out that it took them some seven hours to walk from Jerusalem to Emmaus, but so excited were they by their confrontation with Jesus Christ that that same night they closed the door and started back to share the news with the other disciples. It was not only the news of a living presence in Jesus Christ—"The Lord is risen indeed" (24:34)—but also of a living peace. As they "told about the things that had happened on the road, and how He was known to them in the breaking of bread. . . . Jesus Himself stood in the midst of them, and said to them, 'Peace to you'" (24:36). In verse 49 we note a living power, for they heard the Savior say, "Behold, I send the Promise of My Father upon you; but tarry in the city of Jerusalem until you are endued with power from on high." This consummation meant the warming of the heart, the blessing of the home, the sealing of the happiness of a human life. And when you have the living presence, the living peace, and the living power of Jesus Christ, you have everything you want!

Illustration

Where is happiness? *Not in unbelief*—Voltaire was an infidel of the most pronounced type. He wrote: "I wish I had never been born." *Not in pleasure*—Lord Byron lived a life of pleasure if anyone did. He wrote: "The worm, the canker, and grief are mine alone." *Not in money*—Jay Gould, the American millionaire, had plenty of that. When dying, he said: "I suppose I am the most miserable man on earth." *Not in position and fame*—Lord Beaconsfield enjoyed more than his share of both. He wrote: "Youth is a mistake; manhood a struggle; old age a regret." *Not in military glory*—Alexander the Great conquered the known world in his day. Having done so, he wept in his tent, because he said, "There are no more worlds to conquer." Where then is happiness found?—the answer is simple, in Christ alone.[4]

Conclusion

How far along are you on the journey into joy—conversation, confrontation, or consummation? God has broken into time in Jesus Christ to expose the sadness and slowness of your heart. God has come in Christ along life's journey for this divine confrontation, to face you with the gospel of prophetic, historic, and dynamic truth. You can reject it, or you can swing wide the door of your life and constrain him to come in. God has come that you might know a divine consummation: a satisfied heart, a sanctified home, a sealed happiness. Experience that living presence, that living peace, that living power of Jesus Christ, by constraining him to come in.

Part

Christmas

10

The Wonderful Counselor
Isaiah 9:1–7

"For unto us a Child is born, unto us a Son is given. . . .
And His name will be called Wonderful, Counselor . . ."
(9:6).

Introduction

Isaiah 9:6 is one of the most remarkable prophecies concerning Christ's first coming that we find in Old Testament literature. A careful examination of this verse within its context will reveal that this truth spans the ages. Every dispensation from the beginning of time until the universal reign of Christ is comprehended by these majestic titles of the Lord Jesus Christ. The preexistent Son was born into the human family in order that he might become the wonderful counselor, the mighty God, the everlasting Father, the Prince of Peace. Isaiah uses the words of this prophecy to describe the reign of Christ over a people emancipated out of terrible bondage and unspeakable darkness. The final fulfillment of this great

utterance has yet to be realized when "Jesus shall reign
where'er the sun does his successive journeys run."
Meanwhile, we can know the transforming experience of
Christ in our lives as the wonderful counselor, the mighty
God, the everlasting Father, the Prince of Peace. In this
four-part series on "The Christ of Christmas" we shall
take each of these four great titles and learn something of
the fullness of our gospel and the sufficiency of our glorious Savior.

One of the most popular words of the hour across the
Western world is the term "counselor" or "counseling."
Because of the development of the science of psychology,
together with the pressures and problems of our modern
age, we are becoming people who cannot live without
counselors or counseling.

Some years ago the *New York Herald Tribune* published a series of articles on the subject, "How Mentally
Fit Are We New Yorkers?" In one penetrating article the
writer pointed out that after an eight-year study by a five-
man team at New York Hospital-Cornell Medical Center,
it was concluded that "only one out of five is mentally
well; one out of four is so psychologically disturbed as to
be impaired in his social relations. The rest have some
symptoms of psychological illness but they do not inter-
fere with their lives." The researchers were quick to add,
"The frequency of symptoms does not appear to differ
much from other parts of the United States." In the light
of such facts, how comforting and reassuring to be able to
turn to one who is described as the wonderful counselor.
Isaiah spells out:

I. The Attributes of This Wonderful Counselor

"His name will be called Wonderful, Counselor" (9:6).
The majority of scholars are satisfied to link these two
words together. The term "wonderful" is in itself deeply
suggestive. As someone has said, "It both expresses and

hides the incomprehensible" (F. C. Jennings). Then the thought behind "counselor" is that of one who gives advice and counsel. He is the only one in the universe who requires no counsel himself. So Paul asks, "For who has known the mind of the LORD? Or who has become His counselor?" (Rom. 11:34). The apostle sums up the attributes of this wonderful counselor best when he declares in Colossians 2:2–3, "Christ, in whom are hidden all the treasures of wisdom and knowledge." Note:

A. Christ Is Full of Wisdom

"In whom are hidden all the treasures of wisdom" (Col. 2:3). James tells us that "the wisdom that is from above is first pure, then peaceable, gentle, willing to yield, full of mercy and good fruits, without partiality and without hypocrisy" (James 3:17). What a contrast to the earthly, sensual, and devilish wisdom of the world! Observe carefully that it is described as "wisdom that is . . . pure" (James 3:17). It is not tainted by worldliness or selfish gain. It is not contaminated by our own ideas; rather, it is characterized by the very life, light, and love of God. Anyone can give advice, but how often is their counsel right and pure?

Illustration

A Christian girl went to an unsaved psychiatrist for help with an emotional problem. The psychiatrist, among other things, suggested that she should "throw off all crippling restraints and live it up!" Here was earthly, sensual, and devilish wisdom. When we turn to our wonderful counselor, Jesus Christ, we can always bo oure of wisdom which is pure.

It is *"wisdom that is . . . peaceable"* (James 3:17). When people have the right answer they usually have the wrong attitude. We do not help people by arguing with them. Instead, we set up walls of resentment, frustration, and defeat.

When we turn to Christ he always speaks peace to our disturbed spirits. Indeed, as we follow him throughout the gospels we find him using an often repeated expression, "Go in peace." His last words to his disciples were "Peace I leave with you, My peace I give to you; not as the world gives do I give to you. Let not your heart be troubled, neither let it be afraid" (John 14:27).

But look again. Here is *"wisdom that is . . . gentle, willing to yield"* (James 3:17). As we shall see a little later, Jesus Christ was the most approachable person who ever lived, the perfect gentleman. His enemies had to admit it. Sin-sick souls crowded around him, and little children sought the blessing of his arms. This wonderful counselor never breaks a broken reed or puts out a smoking flax (see Isa. 42:3).

Then observe that this *"wisdom . . . is . . . full of mercy and good fruits"* (James 3:17). Our approach to people is usually critical, overbearing, and unforgiving. Not so when we come to Jesus in all our need and brokenness. He is full of mercy and good fruits. Not only does he forgive our sins, but he regenerates us by his Spirit so that in the place of hatred there is love; in the place of sorrow there is joy; and in the place of unrest there is peace.

Our text goes on to speak of *"wisdom that is . . . without partiality"* (James 3:17). It is humanly impossible to be impartial. However objective we may try to be in making our judgments, invariably our own feelings and prejudices enter into our counseling. But the wisdom from heaven which is embodied in the Lord Jesus Christ never takes sides, except against sin. We can trust him to be utterly fair and just in all his dealings with us.

Finally, we are told that this *"wisdom . . . is . . . without hypocrisy"* (James 3:17). It is free from doubts, wavering, and insincerity. Very often we get advice from people who repudiate their counsel by the rotten lies they are living themselves. This is never true of our wonderful counselor. God is never an actor. When he speaks he does so genuinely, sincerely, and transformingly. What a glorious attribute is this characteristic of wisdom!

B. Christ Is Full of Knowledge

"In whom are hidden all the treasures of . . . knowledge" (Col. 2:3). Knowledge, in this context, has to do with the saving gospel. In other words, Jesus not only knows all about us, but he has the answers to our problems, for in the knowledge of the gospel there is a solution to every problem of life. The darkness of sin is expelled by the entrance of the gospel light. It was Paul who declared, "God who commanded light to shine out of darkness . . . has shone in our hearts to give the light of the knowledge of the glory of God in the face of Jesus Christ" (2 Cor. 4:6).

"Remind the Lord Jesus Christ that as He is Counselor to the church of God, He will be in your particular case Counselor and Guide, and will direct you; and if you wait believingly, expectantly, you will find that the waiting is not in vain, that the Lord will prove Himself a Counselor both wise and good"(George Mueller).

II. The Attractiveness of This Wonderful Counselor

"His name will be called . . . Counselor. . . . Of the increase of His government and peace there will be no end" (9:6 7). Each of the titles in this verse emphasizes the supreme ability of our Savior to administer the government which is placed upon his shoulders. He is going to win all the nations because of his wise and masterful government. Just as the Queen of Sheba came from far to test out the wisdom of Solomon, so people of every tongue and nation under heaven will converge around the throne of the greater Solomon, even Jesus Christ our Lord.

In describing the magnetism of Jesus Christ, Mark says, "They came to Him from every quarter" (Mark 1:45). There was a universal appeal about this wonderful counselor. Indeed, he is the only one in the universe who could stand among men and say, "Come to Me, all you who labor and are heavy laden, and I will give you rest" (Matt. 11:28). Since the mosaic of humanity is totalized in him:

A. He Attracts People Wherever They Are

Prophetic language declares that "to Him shall be the obedience of the people" (Gen. 49:10). It is a historical fact that while the religions of the world have suffered varying fortunes in different parts of the world, Christianity has never failed to strike root wherever the gospel has been worthily preached. Thus Jesus appeals to people everywhere.

B. He Attracts People Whoever They Are

He said, "And I, if I am lifted up from the earth, will draw all peoples to Myself" (John 12:32). Men sought his counsel, women came to him for advice, and little children responded to his welcoming smile. This has been the history of the Christian church ever since this wonderful counselor came into the world.

C. He Attracts People Whatever They Are

"God shows no partiality" (Acts 10:34). Theologians sought his wisdom, sin-sick souls came to him for counsel; and when his enemies attempted to trap him in his words they all came back, saying, "No man ever spoke like this Man!" (John 7:46); "for He taught them as one having authority, and not as the scribes" (Matt. 7:29).

> Who is He the people bless for His words of
>   gentleness?
> Who is He to whom they bring, All the sick and
>   sorrowing?

'Tis the Lord! oh wondrous story!
'Tis the Lord! the King of glory!
At His feet we humbly fall,
Crown Him! crown Him, Lord of all!

                                    Benjamin R. Hanby

III. The Ability of This Wonderful Counselor

"His name will be called Wonderful, Counselor" (9:6).
Some scholars translate this to read, "as a counselor, he
is a wonder"; that is to say, whenever he counsels miracles happen, transformations take place, the supernatural
is seen. This is why there is a sense in which the word
"wonderful" should never be used, except to describe the
wonder-working power of Jesus Christ. Wherever he
extends his governmental counsel there is lasting peace.
As the wonderful counselor:

A. He Has the Ability to Analyze the Condition
of Men and Women

"As a counselor, he is a wonder" beyond all human
perception or comprehension. Take, for example, three
successive chapters in the Gospel of John and watch
him in his analysis of three completely different types
of need.

In John 3 a theological professor came to see him and
started the conversation with a remarkable eulogy:
"Rabbi, we know that You are a teacher come from
God; for no one can do these signs that You do unless
God is with him" (John 3:2). Jesus recognized instantly
that here was a man who had religion without life. In
spite of his theological training and religious influence,
Nicodemus knew nothing about life from above.

Then we turn to chapter 4 and find Jesus speaking
with a woman who knew every trick in the book to
escape analysis; but the Savior saw through her and dis-
cerned that behind her charming and attractive person-

ality was a sordid, frustrated, and defeated sex life. Jesus said to her, "Go, call your husband, and come here" (John 4:16). This at once revealed that she had had five husbands and was now living with a man who was not her husband. Here, then, was a woman with passion but without power. She was helpless when it came to controlling the creative energies locked up inside her.

In John 5 we have a man who suffered with an infirmity for thirty-eight years. Time and again he had sought the healing virtues of the pool of Bethesda but had been disappointed. But when Jesus saw him he detected a sick man without hope. This explains his whole approach when he asked the incredible question, "Do you want to be made well?" (John 5:6).

A study of these three stories is rich with lessons concerning Christ's ability to analyze the condition of men and women. No wonder Jeremiah says, "The heart is deceitful above all things, and desperately wicked; who can know it? I, the LORD, search the heart" (Jer. 17:9–10).

B. He Has the Ability to Apply the Corrective to Men and Women

"As a counselor, he is a wonder." Returning to those three stories again, we notice that Jesus was never satisfied with analyzing people: he always applied the corrective.

How different it is with human means of straightening out lives. While we thank God for Christian psychologists, doctors, and even pastors who are able to provide help to sin-sick souls, there is no guarantee of success. But with Jesus there is never any chance of failure!

To Nicodemus he said, "You must be born again" (John 3:7), and something happened in that man's life, for later he was found at the foot of the cross affectionately overseeing the burial arrangements of the body of Jesus—thus openly confessing his Savior and Lord.

With the woman of Samaria, Jesus said: "If you knew the gift of God, and who it is who says to you, 'Give Me a drink,' you would have asked Him, and He would have given you living water" (John 4:1). The woman accepted his offer: she stooped and drank and lived. Indeed, such was the overflow of this spring of living water in her life that she affected her entire city.

The man with the infirmity was commanded to "Rise, take up your bed and walk." And we read, "Immediately the man was made well" (John 5:8–9).

Amplification

Christ is "wonderful" in his being, in his work, in his ways, and in his words. He can take the sinner sunken in sin and degraded by vice, transform him into an heir of glory, a child of light and holiness. He can take the weak and helpless one and in his own might use him to the pulling down of strongholds. So in his dealings with us in providence, as well as in redemption, how wonderfully he makes the light to shine out of darkness, and the crooked things straight! Let us not be afraid to expect wonders in our life, when we have such a wonderful Savior to undertake for us. It is his delight to reveal to those who trust him the wonders of his love and power and wisdom—as he leads them onward in their walk of faith.

Conclusion

So we see that there is no human malady which Jesus cannot remedy. To become your wonderful counselor, Christ was born at Bethlehem, died at Calvary, and rose triumphantly. Now he waits to change that life of yours. Only he can rid you of your complexes, give you a new life, and be your guide until your journey's end.

The Mighty God
Colossians 1:1–18; Isaiah 9:6

"For unto us a Child is born, unto us a Son is given; . . .
And His name will be called . . . Mighty God" (Isa. 9:6).

Introduction

The second title given to our Lord Jesus Christ is one
of unusual significance. Eminent scholars throughout the
centuries have sought again and again to understand its
full meaning, and the literature which has been written
on the subject is a study in itself. Some have maintained
that the name might be translated "the eradiator" or "the
one who gives light to men." Others have suggested that
the title means "the illustrious" or "the bright and shining one." The majority of Bible students insist that our
English rendering is the best and nearest expression of the
original. In other words, our Lord Jesus Christ is indeed
the mighty one, the strong one, the omnipotent one. Dr.
Alexander Maclaren tells us that the word "mighty"
implies "one who is victorious in battle"—a hero who has

made a name for himself in triumphant warfare. The essential message of this title is that of power, strength, and victory. Thus the prophetic name of the coming Savior reveals:

I. Christ's Power as Creator

"His name will be called . . . Mighty God" (9:6). Centuries later, John interpreted this title by telling us that "in the beginning was the Word, and the Word was with God, and the Word was God. He was in the beginning with God. All things were made through Him, and without Him nothing was made that was made" (John 1:1–3). Paul adds, "For by Him all things were created that are in heaven and that are on earth, visible and invisible, whether thrones or dominions or principalities or powers. All things were created through Him and for Him" (Col. 1:16).

The universe is not self-produced. Biological analysis has failed to show that a single particle of matter can transmute itself into visibility and movement. Furthermore, to create is a personal act; and the divine order and activity seen in creation demands an absolute Being as the first cause of all things. Therefore, as we look at the glory of the heavens and the handiwork of the earth, as we examine the expansiveness of the universe through the telescope and the minuteness of that same universe through the microscope, we have to stand back with adoring worship and declare the mighty God!

Illustration

The famous English deist, Anthony Collins of the 17th century, met a plain countryman one day while out walking. He asked him where he was going. "To church, sir." "What are you going to do there?" "To worship God." "Is your God a great or a little God?" "He is both, sir." "How can he be both?" "He is so great, sir, that the heaven of

heavens cannot contain him; and so little that he can
dwell in my heart." Collins later declared that this simple answer from the countryman had more effect upon
his mind than all the volumes which learned doctors had
written against him. This simple countryman had . . . the
right concept of God, the God of the Bible, who as a
spirit is the Creator of all things and yet indwells the
heart of his believing creatures in the person of Jesus
Christ.[1]

II. Christ's Power as Sustainer

"His name will be called . . . Mighty God" (9:6). The
New Testament expands this by stating: "who being the
brightness of His glory and the express image of His person, and upholding all things by the word of His power,
when He had by Himself purged our sins, sat down at
the right hand of the Majesty on high" (Heb. 1:3); and
again: "He is before all things, and in Him all things con-
sist" (Col. 1:17). Here we are told that not only were all
things created through the word of his power, but they
are sustained and governed by that same power; in other
words, it requires as much power to conserve and to create.

Materialists who attribute the sustained power of creation to "natural laws" cannot prove their position, for to
any thoughtful person it is obvious that laws that have no
power to create even an atom cannot sustain a world. The
truth is that the secret behind all phenomena is the
mighty God. As we look about us we are amazed at this
stupendous fact. No leaf that flutters in the breeze, no
blade of grass that stands erect, consists or holds together
without the sustaining power of the mighty God.

What a concept this is of the one who came to be born
at Bethlehem! Let us remember these lofty views of our
God as Christmas draws near. John Peterson expresses it
well in his hymn of adoration:

All glory to Jesus, begotten of God,
The great I AM is He;
Creator, sustainer—but wonder of all,
The Lamb of Calvary![2]

III. Christ's Power as Redeemer

"His name will be called . . . Mighty God" (9:6). Isaiah beautifully brings these two concepts together when he puts the following words into the mouth of the pre-existent Son: "I, the LORD, am your Savior, and your Redeemer, the Mighty One of Jacob" (Isa. 49:26). As we think through the saving activity of the mighty Son of God, we are impressed with seven aspects of his redeeming work. Consider:

A. Christ's Power to Come to Earth

The prophet tells us, "Unto us a Child is born, unto us a Son is given; and the government will be upon His shoulder. And His name will be called . . . Mighty God" (9:6). The Redeemer's advent was utterly unique. His was a sinless and supernatural birth. He was born of Mary, he was begotten of the Holy Spirit. The message of the angel to this highly favored woman is found in Luke 1:35: "The Holy Spirit will come upon you, and the power of the Highest will overshadow you; therefore, also, that Holy One who is to be born will be called the Son of God." Although Jesus passed through the natural processes of human birth, the conception was initiated by the Holy Spirit. The holy life of the pre-existent Son was united with the seed of the woman and the mighty God was born into the world. Not to believe this is to rob Jesus Christ of his sinless life and his saving virtue. On the other hand, to accept these facts by faith is to kneel worshipfully at his cradle, recognizing his sovereignty in the gift of gold, his deity in the gift of frankincense, and his humanity in the gift of myrrh.

Illustration

Among the thousands throning Trafalgar Square in London every day some doubtless look up in passing at the statue of Lord Nelson on top of its colossal column and try to make out what it is really like. The effort is not easy. In his well-meaning concern to give the famous admiral as exalted a position as possible the sculptor has set him too high to be distinctly discernible from the pavement below; the elevation precludes revelation. At the Ideal Home Exhibition in Olympia in 1948, however, an exact replica in plaster of the figure surmounting the tremendous pillar was placed at eye-level where all could closely examine it, on a balcony of the vast building. Thus for the first time many had an immediate view of the features which before they had only beheld from afar. That is what Jesus did for God. That is the Christmas message. He brought him down, as it were, to our level, within range of our dim finite vision, so that we might see him face to face. At Bethlehem the Most High became the most nigh. "And the Word was made flesh, and dwelt among us, and we beheld His glory" (John 1:14).[3]

B. Christ's Power to Live on Earth

In a most revealing statement found in Romans 1:4, Paul tells us that Jesus Christ was "declared to be the Son of God with power, according to the Spirit of holiness, by the resurrection from the dead." For our purpose, we must content ourselves with observing that the Lord Jesus manifested himself as the mighty God by the spirit of holiness with which he lived in a sinful world. It was because of his sinless life that God raised him from the dead so that his body saw no corruption. It is true that he mingled with sinners, yet the Bible says that he was "holy, harmless, . . . separate from sinners" (Heb. 7:26). It is true that he confronted Satan, but he could testify, "the ruler of this world is coming, and he has nothing in Me" (John 14:30). Throughout his life he was characterized by the spirit of holiness. Only the mighty God could have lived a life of this caliber and quality. This is why Paul, in another of his epistles, declares that the only life worth living is the *life* of the indwelling Son of God (see Gal. 2:20).

C. Christ's Power to Speak on Earth

Again and again throughout the Gospels we read that people "were astonished at His teaching, for He taught them as one having authority, and not as the scribes" (Mark 1:22). No nation in history was more instructed in the theology of religion than the Jewish nation. Patriarchs, potentates, poets, and prophets spoke throughout the centuries; but now one appeared among them who spoke with such authority and power that no one could resist him. In every sense of the word, he spoke as the mighty God. The power of the Savior's utterances were not only unique because of the authority of his statements, but because of the originality of his sources. While the scribes and Pharisees quoted their masters, Jesus stood before men and declared, "You have heard that it was said to those of old, . . . but I say to you" (Matt. 5:21–22). Truly, he was the mighty God!

Amplification

Jesus left no book, no tract, or written page behind him, yet he is more quoted than any writer in all history. His sayings at times are on almost every tongue, and his words have literally gone out into all the world. No man ever laid down his life in Asia or in Africa to translate Plato or Aristotle, Kant or Hegel, Shakespeare or Milton, but hundreds have died to carry Jesus' priceless words to the ends of the earth. Several hundred languages have been reduced to writing in order to transmit his life-giving message. Savage tribes have been uplifted, cannibals civilized, head-hunters converted, schools and colleges founded, and the character and culture of individuals and of peoples have been changed as the result of the influence of his words which are creative spirit and life.[4]

D. Christ's Power to Work on Earth

When the two disciples on the way to Emmaus were reviewing the ministry of the Lord Jesus, they summed it up by saying he was "a Prophet *mighty* in deed and word before God and all the people" (Luke 24:19). Supernatural power and strength, which could not be denied, were demonstrated in all that he did. When he healed the sick the people cried, "He has done all things well" (Mark 7:37). When he miraculously fed the hungry it is recorded that onlookers said, "This is truly the Prophet who is to come into the world" (John 6:14). When he stilled the waves his disciples "marveled, saying, 'Who can this be, that even the winds and the sea obey Him?'" (Matt. 8:27). When he exorcised the demon out of a mute man "the multitudes marveled, saying, 'It was never seen like this in Israel!'" (Matt. 9:33). When he forgave sinners "the multitudes . . . marveled and glorified God, who had given such power to men" (Matt. 9:8).

E. Christ's Power to Die on Earth

Man is born to live; Jesus came to die. This is why Jesus declared, "Therefore My Father loves Me, because I lay down My life that I may take it again. No one takes it from Me, but I lay it down of Myself. I have power to lay it down" (John 10:17–18). This is one of the most remarkable statements Jesus Christ ever made on earth to describe the character of his death. Notice it was voluntary as to *motive.* With the cross before him he could say, "the Son of Man did not come to be served, but to serve, and to give His life a ransom for many" (Matt. 20:28); and again: "for this purpose I came to this hour" (John 12:27). Even more amazing, Christ's death was voluntary as to *method.* While he escaped lynching and stoning a number of times, he could tell his disciples with complete composure that he would be delivered to the Gentiles to be mocked, scourged, and crucified (see

Matt. 20:19). Perhaps the most astonishing aspect of this truth is the fact that his death was voluntary as to the *moment.* When the hour struck he bowed his head and gave up his spirit (see John 19:30).

This voluntary character of the death of Christ lifts it out of the realm of ordinary deaths into the place of uniqueness, infinite wonder, and redemptive significance. It is not surprising, therefore, that a hardened centurion standing by the cross exclaimed, "Truly this Man was the Son of God!" (Mark 15:39). Needless to say, only such a death could redeem sinners like you and me.

Illustration

It was during the funeral procession of Abraham Lincoln that a humble black mother, standing respectfully behind the crowd of white people, held her baby high above her head as the martyred president's body passed, and said, "Take a long look at him, son; that's the man who died for you." To look unto Christ who died for you is to receive life, to find cleansing from sin, to discover a motive for the defeat of temptation. Christian, take a long look at him today; he's the man who died for you.[5]

F. Christ's Power to Rise on Earth

He said, "I have power to lay [My life] . . . down, and I have power to take it again . . ." (John 10:18). Now the Bible records a number of stories of people who were raised to life; but to be absolutely accurate in our definition, all such persons were resuscitated rather than raised from the dead. The proof of this is that they died again. Dr. F. B. Meyer said in one of his sermons, "These people had one cradle, but two coffins." But when Jesus rose from the dead he conquered death forever: "Death no longer has dominion over Him" (Rom. 6:9); he is "alive forevermore" (Rev. 1:18). So in the resurrection of Jesus Christ the omnipotence of God was manifested, proving he was and is the mighty God.

Illustration

The resurrection of Jesus Christ is the cornerstone of the Christian faith. Without it the believer has no hope for this life or for the life to come. Our belief in this great teaching is not based upon some religious feeling or upon an unfounded idea about what may have happened in the past. Nor are we talking about an isolated rumor, but about a historical fact with solid evidence to support it. In the early part of this century, a group of lawyers met in England to discuss the biblical accounts of Jesus' resurrection. They wanted to see if sufficient information was available to make a case that would hold up in an English court of law. When their study was completed they published the results of their investigation. They concluded that Christ's resurrection was one of the most well-established facts of history![6]

G. Christ's Power to Save on Earth

When Jesus was still here in the flesh he could say, "The Son of Man has power on earth to forgive sins" (Matt. 9:6). This forgiving and saving ministry continues through his mediatorial office as intercessor. The writer to the Hebrews puts it this way: "He is . . . able to save to the uttermost those who come to God through Him, since he ever lives to make intercession for them" (Heb. 7:25). What a glorious gospel this is! It includes salvation from the penalty of sin, the power of sin, and, one day, from the presence of sin. Here is salvation in all its fullness and completeness. Every aspect of God's redeeming purpose is included in that phrase, "able to save to the uttermost" (Heb. 7:25). It matters not who or what you are: the mighty God can save you. If you are a religious sinner he can save you; if you are a pagan sinner he can save you; if you are an intellectual sinner he can save you; if you are an ignorant sinner he can save you; if you are a cultured sinner he can save you; if you are a depraved sinner he can save you. The truth of this text in Hebrews is all-inclusive: it embraces everyone.

Conclusion

What a glorious Christmas message this is to a world waiting in the shadow of darkness and death: "His name will be called . . . Mighty God" (9:6)—mighty as Creator, Sustainer, Redeemer. Will you claim him as your Redeemer here and now?

12

The Everlasting Father
Revelation 1:19–20; Isaiah 9:6

"For unto us a Child is born, unto us a Son is given. . . .
His name will be called . . . Everlasting Father" (Isa. 9:6).

Introduction

The name "everlasting Father" is perhaps the most
mysterious and puzzling of the four titles that are accord-
ed our blessed Lord in this remarkable prophecy of
Isaiah. As C. H. Spurgeon remarks, "How complex is the
person of our Lord Jesus Christ! Almost in the same
breath the prophet calls Him 'a Child,' 'a son,' 'a Counselor,' and 'a Father.'" The more we look into this title,
the greater becomes the unfoldings of divine truth concerning this glorious Savior of mankind. One thing we
should make clear from the very start is that this title has
reference to the second person of the Trinity and not to
God the Father. The Son is not the Father, neither is the
Father the Son—though they are essentially and eternally
co-equal. The title is rather designed to describe a glori-

ous aspect of the ministry of the Lord Jesus which is well supported throughout the rest of Scripture. As everlasting Father, he is:

I. The Final Head of a New Revelation

"His name will be called . . . Everlasting Father" (9:6). John tells us that "no one has seen God at any time. The only begotten Son, who is in the bosom of the Father, He has declared Him" (John 1:18). The Father-heart of God would never have been revealed to mankind had not the Lord Jesus come to live among men as the revelation of the Father. It is true that, to some degree, the fatherhood of God was known in Old Testament times by patriarchs, priests, poets, and prophets who ever looked onward to a final revelation. The Hebrew writer expresses it perfectly: "God, who at various times and in different ways spoke in time past to the fathers by the prophets has in these last days spoken to us by His Son" (Heb. 1:1–2). So in knowing the Lord Jesus Christ we are introduced to the nature and character of the everlasting Father. Again John writes: "He who has seen Me has seen the Father" (John 14:9).

Now there are three all-inclusive revelations of God the Father which Jesus Christ came to interpret to men:

A. The Father of Eternal Life

In his prologue John reminds us that "in the beginning was the Word, and the Word was with God, and the Word was God. . . . In Him was life" (John 1:1, 4). Throughout his entire ministry Jesus was ever speaking of this eternal life. Indeed, at least forty-five times in the New Testament this life is spoken of as God's supreme gift to all who believe. For example, the Savior stood among men and announced, "I have come that they may have life, and that they may have it more abundantly." This was eternal life in its quantitative measure. But Jesus also added, "I give them eternal life,

and they shall never perish; neither shall anyone
snatch them out of My hand" (John 10:10, 28). This
was eternal life in its qualitative measure. So as the revelation of the Father of eternity, the Christ of Christmas
brought eternal life to a human race "dead in trespasses
and . . . sins" (Eph. 2:1).

Illustration

Dr. Walter Wilson once visited in a home where the
members of the family were asked to quote Bible verses.
One little girl quoted John 3:16 as follows: "For God so
loved the world, that he gave his only begotten Son, that
whosoever believeth in him, should not perish but have
internal life." Needless to say, he did not correct her, for it
is internal life, as well as everlasting life.[1]

B. The Father of Eternal Light

"In Him was life, and the life was the light of men"
(John 1:4). Later the Master could add, "I am the light
of the world. He who follows Me shall not walk in
darkness, but have the light of life" (John 8:12). As eternal light, Jesus revealed every aspect of the holiness,
righteousness, and justice of God the Father. At the
same time He exposed every aspect of the wickedness,
lawlessness, and sinfulness of man. Men and demons
tried to extinguish that light but never succeeded. Out
of the darkness and gloom of Calvary the light shone
when Christ the Son of God cried, "It is finished!"
(John 19:30). He was buried, but the light shone on, for
the third day he arose as "the Sun of Righteousness
with healing in His wings" (Mal. 4:2). The Bible tells
us that "God is light" (1 John 1:5). This fact has been
revealed supremely in the person of the Lord Jesus.

Illustration

Bob Woods, in *Pulpit Digest,* tells the story of a couple
who took their son, 11, and daughter, 7, to Carlsbad Cav-
erns. As always, when the tour reached the deepest point

in the cavern, the guide turned off all the lights to drama-
tize how completely dark and silent it is below the earth's
surface. The little girl, suddenly enveloped in utter darkness, was frightened and began to cry. Immediately was
heard the voice of her brother: "Don't cry. Somebody here
knows how to turn on the lights." In a real sense, that is
the message of the gospel: light is available. It is Jesus
shining in the midst of the world's darkness.[2]

C. The Father of Eternal Love

"No one has seen God at any time. The only begotten Son, who is in the bosom of the Father, He has
declared Him" (John 1:18). Could words better describe
the revelation of the heart of God? He came from the
very bosom of the Father to tell a lost world that "God
so loved the world that He gave His only begotten Son,
that whoever believes in Him should not perish but
have everlasting life" (John 3:16). Such sacrificial love
involved the accomplishment of an eternal redemption
for you and for me. So the writer to the Hebrews says,
"With His own blood He entered the Most Holy Place
once for all, having obtained eternal redemption" (Heb.
9:12). Because of that eternal redemption we have an
eternal salvation, for "having been perfected, He
became the author of eternal salvation to all who obey
Him" (Heb. 5:9). "God is love" (1 John 4:8). This is what
distinguishes the Christian conception of a heavenly
Father from all other religions of the world. How wonderful, then, that he came into this world as the everlasting Father!

II. The Founder-Head of a New Religion

James speaks of "pure and undefiled religion before
God and the Father" (James 1:27). Without doubt, Jesus
was the Father and founder of this. The Hebrews were in
the habit of calling a man father of the thing which he

invented. For instance, Jubal is called "the father of all those who play the harp and flute" (Gen. 4:21); and Jabal "was the father of those who dwell in tents and have livestock" (Gen. 4:20). Later in history, men followed this custom in naming certain great men as the fathers (or founders) of their particular science or system. For instance, Socrates was called "the father of philosophy"; Galen was named "the father of medicine"; whereas Herodotus has been known through the centuries as "the father of history." In a very real sense, therefore, we can talk about Christ as the founder-head of a new religion, or "the founder of Christianity." The New Testament reveals that this new religion is characterized by:

A. The Word of the Father

James exhorts that we are to "be doers of the word, and not hearers only" (James 1:22). We know that the Lord Jesus was the Word, and brought the Word of the Father to this world. "The law was given through Moses, but grace and truth came through Jesus Christ" (John 1:17). He declared, "I am . . . the truth" (John 14:6)—not only incarnate truth, but the author of inspired truth, as we have it in the Bible. Paul tells us that "all Scripture is given by inspiration of God, and is profitable for doctrine, for reproof, for correction, for instruction in righteousness" (2 Tim. 3:16). There is no other safe guide in matters of faith and life outside the covers of the Book we call the Holy Scriptures. The manifesto of heaven for life on earth was introduced into this world by Jesus Christ. In this sense he is the founder-head of a new religion, for he not only included the Law and the prophets of an old economy, but transcended them.

Amplification

Truth is exclusive, it denies and shuts out its opposite. The greater the truth the greater the realm in which it refuses rivalry. So Christ, as Savior, stands alone. He is God and no other voice can tell us anything about God. He alone is the way and the truth.[3]

B. The Work of the Father

"Pure and undefiled religion before God and the Father is this: to visit orphans and widows in their trouble, and to keep oneself unspotted from the world" (James 1:27). James is here restating the truth which our Lord enunciated regarding the day of judgment when he would recognize those who rendered him service, and those who withheld service (see Matt. 25:36–43). In fact, "James uses precisely the same word here for 'visit' . . . when he says that pure religion and undefiled in the eyes of the Father-God is to *visit* those who are bereft of human fathers."[4] God himself is revealed in the Bible as "a father of the fatherless, a defender of widows" (Ps. 68:5); and again: "When my father and my mother forsake me, then the LORD will take care of me" (Ps. 27:10). It is certainly pertinent to remember that one of Christ's strongest condemnations was addressed to Pharisees who enriched themselves at the expense of the helpless—especially widows (see Mark 12:40). In this way the Lord Jesus manifested the Father's heart in what James calls "pure religion." God made us "pure and undefiled" in this respect.

III. The Federal Head of a New Race

Paul tells us that the Lord Jesus is "the firstborn among many brethren" (Rom. 8:29). This means that Christ's rank as firstborn declares him to be the exalted head of a new humanity. The apostle develops this important theme in 1 Corinthians 15 where he reminds us: "As in Adam all die, even so in Christ all shall be made alive" (v. 22). Adam was the federal head of all living, but by his fall he ruined us all. God said to him, "In the day that you eat of [the fruit] . . . you shall surely die" (Gen. 2:17). In that death he incurred the death of the human race. Romans 5:12 tells us: "As through one man sin entered the world, and death through sin, . . . thus death spread to all men, because all sinned." In Adam all die; in Christ shall all be made alive. Jesus is the last Adam, and by union with this federal head we become partakers of a new nature and a redeemed humanity. While generation makes us sons of Adam, regeneration makes us sons of God. In this sense Christ is the everlasting Father.

If the question be asked as to how this miracle takes place, then John gives us the answer when he says, "As many as received Him, to them He gave the right to become children of God, even to those who believe in His name: who were born, not of blood, nor of the will of the flesh, nor of the will of man, but of God" (John 1:12–13). Our entry into this new humanity is not by human descent—it is "not of blood," nor of human desire—"not of . . . flesh"; nor of human design—not "of the will of man" (John 1:13): it is an act of God in Christ. This miracle is effected when we:

A. Believe the Everlasting Father

"To them He gave the right to become children of God, even to those who believe in His name" (John 1:12). As the eternal Word, the Lord Jesus was also the everlasting Father—the Father of eternity; therefore, the Father of eternal life, love, and light. To believe all this is the first great step into this miracle of regeneration and new birth. It must be more than head knowledge; there must be belief with the heart.

B. Receive the Everlasting Father

"As many as received Him, to them He gave the right to become children of God" (John 1:12). This is an act of the mind, the heart, and the will whereby Jesus Christ, as the very Father of eternity, is received into the human personality. Just as he was born a little babe in Bethlehem, so he must be born again in your heart and mine. Nothing less than this transaction makes us children of the everlasting Father and, therefore, united to the federal head of a new race.

Illustration

W. Y. Fullerton recalls his futile attempts to begin the Christian life. One Sunday morning he made up his mind to be a Christian, and never doubted that he knew what to do. He would leave off this evil thing—already evil things had a place in his life—he must do this good thing, read his Bible more, pray more, repent, and weep if possible; that evidently was the proper way. So he began. On Sunday he prospered well, on Monday and Tuesday he almost succeeded, but on Wednesday and Thursday he made some serious slips. By Friday he gave up in despair, but started in earnest again on Sunday. In his self-confidence he thought he knew where he had gone wrong, and he would try to guard against the danger. So he read his Bible more diligently and prayed with increasing devotion (at times falling asleep on his knees beside the bed). He watched more carefully and imagined he repented more deeply. Often he wept and hid the tears. Then came the wonderful Sunday afternoon when the new minister was to give his first address to the Sunday school. Fullerton remembered just one sentence of all he said, but it was just what he needed to hear: "All you have to do to be saved is to take God's gift, and say 'Thank you.'" Here was a new and great light. Before he had been trying to get God to take his gift, trying to make it great enough to be worthy of his acceptance; now it was Fullerton who had to simply take the gift that was offered him. Quietly that Sunday afternoon his heart turned to God, and he took the gift for which ever after he said "Thank you."[5]

Conclusion

Have you received the Lord Jesus Christ into your life? Or is your answer, "I have no room for him."

No room for the Baby at Bethlehem's inn,
Only a cattle shed.
No home on earth for the dear Son of God,
Nowhere to lay His head.
Only a cross did they give to our Lord,
Only a borrowed tomb.
Today He is seeking a place in your heart,
Will you still say to Him, "No room"?

Rather, may your response be:

O come to my heart, Lord Jesus!
There is room in my heart for Thee.

Emily E. S. Elliott

The Prince of Peace

Isaiah 9:2–7

"For unto us a Child is born, unto us a Son is given. . . . And His name will be called . . . Prince of Peace" (9:6).

Introduction

Of the four titles given to our Lord Jesus Christ in Isaiah's prophecy this one is the greatest, for it speaks to the deepest needs of the human heart. Peace was the supreme longing of the true Israelite and was the promised fulfillment of the Messiah's reign: so they sang and sighed for the coming Prince of Peace.

What was true of that prophetic age is equally relevant to our war-ridden generation. Could anything be more welcome in this hour of unrest, conflict, and bloodshed than the coming of the Prince of Peace? The fact of the matter is that there will be no peace personally or generally until Christ is welcomed and enthroned. Let us then examine this glorious title and learn what the Holy Spirit has to say to us from this combination of words. Observe that the title "Prince of Peace" represents:

I. The Author of Peace

"And His name will be called . . . Prince of Peace" (9:6). There are no less than fifteen different Hebrew words that are translated "prince" in the King James Version. Basically, however, the idea behind the word is that of "ruler," "leader," and "captain"—though its Greek translation adds the further thought of "author" and "pioneer." It is quite obvious, from the unfolding of divine revelation, that the Lord Jesus came into the world in order that he might make peace, give peace, and preach peace.

A. Jesus Brought Peace at His Birth

The angelic announcement was "Glory to God in the highest, and on earth peace, good will toward men!" (Luke 2:14). Never was there a time in history when the hour was more propitious for the coming of Christ into the world. The apostle Paul writes, "When the fullness of the time had come, God sent forth His Son" (Gal. 4:4). World conditions were ripe for God's supreme act in his redemptive purpose. Search the pages of history and in all the story of the centuries you will not find any generation in which the Savior could better have come than the one in which he did come.

Illustration

During the long war years a boy looked frequently at a picture of his daddy on the table. He had left when the boy was a young infant. After several years the boy had forgotten him as a person, but he would often look at the picture and say, "If only my father could step out of that picture and be real." Christmas means that in a sad day of sin, when man had almost forgotten God, he stepped into the world in the form of his Son, and angels announced, "Peace on earth" (see Luke 2:14).[1]

B. Jesus Taught Peace in His Life

He could look into the faces of men and women and say, "These things I have spoken to you, that in Me you may have peace. In the world you will have tribulation; but be of good cheer, I have overcome the world" (John 16:33); and again: "Peace I leave with you, My peace I give to you; not as the world gives do I give to you. Let not your heart be troubled, neither let it be afraid" (John 14:27). That which attracted men and women to him was not only his word of peace, but also his way of peace. In his life they could discern a composure, a calm and tranquility which was utterly removed from the worried and harassed looks of the religious teachers of that day. They saw him silence storms, exorcise demons, heal diseases, and speak peace to those who were beaten by sin. Again and again his message to those who came to him was "Go in peace" (Mark 5:34; Luke 8:48).

Illustration

A reporter asked the late President Herbert Hoover, "Mr. President, how do you handle criticism? Do you ever get agitated or tense?" "No," President Hoover said, seemingly surprised at the question, "of course not." "But," the reporter went on, "when I was a boy you were one of the most popular men in the world. Then for a while you became one of the most unpopular, with nearly everyone against you. Didn't any of this meanness and criticism ever get under your skin?" "No, I knew when I went into politics what I might expect, so when it came I wasn't disappointed or upset," he said. He lowered his familiar bushy eyebrows and looked directly into the reporter's eyes. "Besides, I have 'peace at the center,'" he added. Inner peace comes from looking to God, our source. Peace is the gift of Jesus Christ. Jesus, before leaving his disciples, said, "Peace I leave with you, My peace I give to you" (John 14:27).[2]

C. Jesus Bought Peace by His Death

"Having made peace through the blood of His cross" (Col. 1:20); that is to say, he paid the price for man's reconciliation to God. With the human race alienated from a holy God, Jesus Christ established an honorable peace by his birth, life, and death. He slew the enmity which prevented peace, and by his mighty redemptive work he made a peace available which the world cannot give or take away. Have we entered into this experience of peace with God through our Lord Jesus Christ?

II. The Arbitrator of Peace

"And the government will be upon His shoulder. And His name will be called . . . Prince of Peace" (9:6). In his Epistle to the Colossians, the apostle has a very remarkable interpretation of this aspect of truth concerning the Prince of Peace. Exhorting the believers to forbear and forgive one another, Paul climaxes his instruction with the words, "And let the peace of God [more literally, the peace of Christ] rule in your hearts" (Col. 3:15). Professor F. F. Bruce points out that the word "rule" here is better translated "arbitrate." The fact of the matter is that wherever the government of Jesus Christ is welcomed and honored peace arbitrates and rules, for "He Himself is our peace" (Eph. 2:14). This is true of:

A. The Personal Life of the Christian

"Let the word of Christ [arbitrate] . . . in your hearts" (Col. 3:15). Undoubtedly, the first application of this exhortation is to the individual believer. It is pointless to talk about peace in the church if there is no peace in the hearts of individual believers. Such peace, of course, comes through receiving and enthroning the Lord Jesus Christ as Prince of Peace within the heart and life. Where he reigns with undisputed authority the Spirit of God and the Word of God extend the peace of God to every area of the life. In other words, the Holy Spirit cannot produce the fruit of peace, nor can the Word of God extend the rule of peace, if there are areas which are not conquered by the indwelling presence of Christ. Only when his government is increased will the peace also be increased.

Illustration

When George V was crowned King of Britain, his eldest son went to the old Welsh castle of Carnarvon to be received as the Prince of Wales. Accompanied by David Lloyd George, the great Welsh statesman, he approached the castle door. All within was still. The door was closed and barred. He knocked, but there was no answer. Again he knocked, with no answer. He knocked a third time. The bar was drawn, the door was flung wide open, and, as he entered, the castle was glorious with light, and the hall was vocal with song. "Lift up your heads, O ye gates; and be ye lift up, ye everlasting doors; and the King of glory shall come in" (Ps. 24:7 KJV). Open the door today, and begin rejoicing in the presence of heaven's crown prince, the Lord Jesus Christ.[3]

B. The General Life of the Church

"Let the peace of God [arbitrate] . . . in your hearts, to which also you were called in one body; and be thankful" (Col. 3:15). This is highly significant. The arbitrating peace of God is not only to affect the individual life of the Christian, but the general life of the church by smoothing out the differences and conflicts that arise in the body. This is what Paul means when he says, "endeavoring to keep the unity of the Spirit in the bond of peace" (Eph. 4:3); and again: "As much as depends on you, live peaceably with all men" (Rom. 12:18). By allowing Christ to reign supremely as Prince of Peace in our hearts we actually contribute to the elimination of discord within the church and, more essentially, to the harmony and true functioning of the body of Christ on earth. The most outstanding evidence of the presence of the supernatural in the church is that of unity. This was the burden of our Savior before he went to heaven. He prayed "that they all may be one . . . that the world may believe that You sent Me" (John 17:21). The psalmist reminds us: "How good and how pleasant it is for brethren to dwell together in unity! . . . For there the LORD commanded the blessing—life forevermore" (Ps. 133:1, 3).

Illustration

In his book *The Mark of the Christian,* Francis Schaeffer told that Hitler, during World War II, ordered the union of all religious denominations in Germany. A Brethren group became deeply divided over the issue. One segment obeyed and suffered little persecution, but gradually their spiritual vitality was weakened. The group that resisted stayed vibrant, but many died in the concentration camps due to their stand. Following the war, feelings between these groups were sharp. Tensions were high. An elder of one of the groups told Francis Schaeffer that they knew the problem had to be resolved. So leaders of both groups agreed to get alone in a quiet place to ask God to show each one where he had failed to keep Christ's commands. After several days of heart-searching, they met together. "And what happened then?" asked Schaeffer. "We just were one!" the elder replied.[4]

Have we accepted the government of the Lord Jesus in our lives? Remember, the government he wants to establish and exercise in our lives rests upon his shoulder—the shoulder that once carried the cross to Calvary. We will never know peace until we recognize Jesus as the author and arbitrator of peace in our hearts and lives.

III. The Authenticator of Peace

"His name will be called . . . Prince of Peace. Of the increase of His government and peace there will be no end, upon the throne of David and over His kingdom, to order it and establish it" (9:6–7). Now while it is possible to know peace in the personal life of the Christian, and the general life of the church here and now, there is an actual age of peace yet to be established at the coming again of the Prince of Peace. There are two ways in which the Prince of Peace authenticates peace:

A. The Millennial Age of Peace

"Of the increase of His government and peace there will be no end" (9:7). When the church (consisting of all genuine believers regardless of denominational affiliation), has gone to meet the Lord in the air, certain events will follow which will usher in what is known as the millennium, or one thousand years of peaceful rule.

First, there will be the emergence of the Antichrist who will reign for seven years with tyranny and terror. This period will conclude with the dread conflict of Armageddon when he, who is the King of Kings and Lord of Lords, will engage the massed armies of the Antichrist and consume the man of sin "with the breath of His mouth and destroy with the brightness of His coming" (2 Thess. 2:8). The troops gathered in opposition to the Son of God will be scattered and left on the battlefield to be devoured by the birds of prey (see Rev. 19:21). Then Jesus will reign as Prince of Peace. He will establish his kingdom on earth and extend his government and peace to the ends of the world.

The prophets of the Old Testament looked across the centuries and described vividly the glories and excellencies of this kingdom where peace, order, and justice will prevail (see Isa. 9.0–7). They foretold a day when "Nation shall not lift up sword against nation, neither shall they learn war any more" (Mic. 4:3). They described the hour when "righteousness will leave the scaffold and once more mount the throne" (see Isa. 11:1–9); when "the earth shall be full of the knowledge of the LORD as the waters cover the sea" (Isa. 11:9), and when prosperity will be the order of the day. What a glorious hope for those who are united by faith to the

Prince of Peace! Are you ready for that millennial reign of Christ?

B. The Eternal Age of Peace

"Of the increase of His government and peace there will be no end" (9:7). Implicit in the words of this text is something that goes beyond the thousand years of the millennial reign of Christ. Prophetic Scripture teaches that at the end of this glorious reign there will be a sad but brief interlude, namely, Satan's final ineffective effort to thwart the purposes of God (see Rev. 20:7–10). But, once again, the enemy of God will be overcome and consigned to the bottomless pit. The great white throne will be set up and the doom of all unbelievers will be forever sealed (see Rev. 20:11–15). Then the new heavens and the new earth will replace the old heaven and the old earth by a process of a mighty, fiery convulsion which Peter describes in his second epistle (see 2 Peter 3:12–13), and God will be all in all. The long, sad record of man's treachery and rebellion will have come to an end, and peace will be established for ever and for ever. Anticipating that day, Peter says, "Therefore, beloved, looking forward to these things, be diligent to be found by Him in peace, without spot and blameless" (2 Peter 3:14).

Illustration

One evening in the dark war days of 1940 Anthony Eden (Lord Avon, as he became) and Winston Churchill were dining alone. They were sitting debating which period of history they would have preferred to live in, had the choice been theirs. Churchill favored the age of Queen Anne and Marlborough's wars. Eden preferred that of Pitt and the struggle with Napoleon. They were both attracted by the first Elizabethan Age. After they had been talking in this fashion for awhile, Churchill concluded: "Of course, of all of them this is the greatest! This is the one in which to live!" And he meant it. . . . Nevertheless, as Browning said, "the best is yet to be." Earth's finest age lies not in the past but in the future—the millennial age in which Jesus Christ will personally preside over the affairs of this planet. And—wondrous thought!—every trueborn child of God will be alive on earth at that time![5]

Conclusion

When we sing about the Prince of Peace in Handel's oratorio, the *Messiah,* let us remember that that title represents the author of peace, the arbitrator of peace, and the authenticator of peace. If we are to be sharers in all that is implied and involved in this title we must open our whole being to this Prince of Peace who came at Christmastime to make peace, give peace, and preach peace.

> The Prince of Peace came down to earth,
> To bring "peace and good will";
> The angels sang with joy and mirth,
> On Beth'lem's silent hill.
>
> The prince of Peace died on the cross,
> To "make peace through His blood";
> He died to save us from our loss,
> And give us "peace with God."
>
> The Prince of Peace rose from the grave,
> To "preach peace" to us all,
> For in that word is pow'r to save,
> When on His name we call.
>
> The Prince of Peace now reigns above,
> To give peace to each soul;
> And he who yields to Him in love,
> Is instantly made whole.
>
> O, Prince of Peace! descend we pray,
> And in us live and stay:
> Cast out our sin, and have full sway,
> Until th' eternal day.

Stephen F. Olford

Endnotes

Introduction

1. *The Wycliffe Bible Commentary,* ed. by Charles F. Pfeiffer (O.T.) and Everett F. Harrison (N.T.). (Chicago: Moody Press, 1962), p. 619.

2. Ilion T. Jones, *Principles and Practice of Preaching* (New York: Abingdon-Cokesbury Press, 1956), pp. 93–99.

Chapter 1

1. *Gospel Herald,* quoted in Walter B. Knight, *3,000 Illustrations for Christian Service* (Grand Rapids: Eerdmans, 1952), pp. 592–93.

2. *Sunday Circle,* quoted in ibid., p. 583, adapted.

3. From the book *The Charles L. Allen Treasury* by Charles L. Wallis, ed., copyright © 1970 by Fleming H. Revell Company, p. 19. Used by permission of Fleming H. Revell Company.

Chapter 2

1. Adapted and reprinted from *The Word for Every Day* by Alvin N. Rogness, copyright © 1981 Augsburg Publishing House, p. 11. Used by permission of Augsburg Fortress.

2. *The Pulpit Commentary,* Gospel of John, p. 143.

3. Lloyd John Ogilvie, *Congratulations—God Believes in You* (Waco: Word, 1980), pp. 102–3, adapted.

Chapter 3

1. Paul Harvey, *The Rest of the Story* (New York: Doubleday, 1977), pp. 74–75, adapted.

2. Eugenia Price, *The Burden Is Light* (New York: Doubleday, 1982), pp. 92–93.

3. Herbert Vander Lugt, *Our Daily Bread* (Grand Rapids: Radio Bible Class).

Chapter 4

1. S. D. Gordon, quoted in Walter B. Knight, *Knight's Master Book of New Illustrations* (Grand Rapids: Eerdmans, 1956), p. 418.

2. Paul Lee Tan, *Encyclopedia of 7,700 Illustrations* (Dallas: Bible Communications, 1979), p. 698, adapted.

3. Knight, *Knight's Master Book of New Illustrations,* p. 419, adapted.

Chapter 5

1. Kenneth G. Hanna, "Hardships Are Heavensent," *Moody Monthly* (Nov. 1984), p. 42.

2. From the book *Living the Lord's Prayer* by Everett Fullam, copyright 1980 by Everett Fullam, pp. 27–28. Published by Chosen Books, Fleming H. Revell Company. Used by permission.

Chapter 6

1. C. Truman Davis, *The Crucifixion of Jesus,* pp. 186–87, adapted from *The Expositor's Bible Commentary,* ed. Frank E. Gaebelein, vol. 8 (Grand Rapids: Zondervan, 1984), p. 779.

2. Stephen F. Olford, *The Secret of Soul-Winning* (Chicago: Moody Press, 1963), pp. 84–85, adapted.

Chapter 7

1. Walter B. Knight, *Knight's Master Book of New Illustrations* (Grand Rapids: Eerdmans, 1956), pp. 155–56, adapted.

2. *Our Daily Bread* (Grand Rapids: Radio Bible Class), adapted.

Chapter 8

1. *Sunday School Times,* quoted in Walter B. Knight, *3,000 Illustrations for Christian Service* (Grand Rapids: Eerdmans, 1952), p. 271.

2. Paul Lee Tan, *Encyclopedia of 7,700 Illustrations* (Dallas: Bible Communications, 1979), p. 1526, adapted.

3. Ted S. Rendall, "By Calvary Love Controlled," *The Prairie Overcomer* (April 1983), p. 204, adapted.

Chapter 9

1. Leon Morris, *The Gospel According to St. Luke,* Tyndale New Testament Commentaries (Grand Rapids: Eerdmans,1960), pp. 338–39.

2. David C. Egner, *Our Daily Bread* (Grand Rapids: Radio Bible Class, April 19, 1984), adapted.

3. J. B. Tweter, quoted in Walter B. Knight, *Knight's Master Book of New Illustrations* (Grand Rapids: Eerdmans, 1956), p. 512, adapted.

4. *The Bible Friend,* quoted in Paul Lee Tan, *Encyclopedia of 7,700 Illustrations* (Dallas: Bible Communications, 1979), p. 682.

Chapter 11

1. Quoted in *Pulpit Helps* (Chattanooga, Tenn.: AMG International, Dec. 1984), p. 30.

2. Copyright 1957. Renewed 1985 by John W. Peterson Music Company. All rights reserved. International copyright secured. Used by permission.

3. *Prophetic Witness,* vol. 10, no. 12 (Loughborough, England: Prophetic Witness Movement International, Dec. 1986), p. 9.

4. Sherwood Eddy, quoted in *Pulpit Helps* (Chattanooga, Tenn.: AMG International, Dec. 1984), p. 31.

5. G. Franklin Allee, *Evangelistic Illustrations for Pulpit and Platform* (Chicago: Moody, 1961), p. 61.

6. *Sermons Illustrated* (Holland, Ohio: May 13, 1986).

Chapter 12

1. Paul Lee Tan, *Encyclopedia of 7,700 Illustrations* (Dallas: Bible Communications, 1979), p. 441.

2. Adapted from *Leadership,* vol. 7, no. 2 (Spring 1986), p. 47.

3. Paul Rader, "Who Is Truth?" *Reality,* vol. 12, no. 9 (Sept. 1984), p. 3.

4. See R. V. G. Tasker, *The General Epistle of James,* Tyndale New Testament Commentaries (Grand Rapids: Eerdmans, 1979), p. 55.

5. Walter B. Knight, *3,000 Illustrations for Christian Service* (Grand Rapids: Eerdmans, 1952), p. 583, adapted.

Chapter 13

1. *Pulpit Helps* (Chattanooga, Tenn.: AMG International, Dec. 1984), p. 7.

2. *Sermons Illustrated* (Holland, Ohio: Dec. 25, 1985).

3. T. S. Rendall, "Rejoice! The Prince Is Born," *The Prairie Overcomer,* vol. 55, no. 8 (Dec. 1982), p. 591.

4. Dennis J. DeHaan, *Our Daily Bread* (Grand Rapids: Radio Bible Class, Dec. 15, 1985).

5. *Prophetic Witness,* vol. 6, no. 9 (Loughborough, England: Prophetic Witness Movement International, Sept. 1982), p. 13.

For Further Reading

Part 1: Good Friday and Easter

Bininger, Clem E. *The Seven Last Words of Christ.* Grand Rapids: Baker Book House, 1969.

Blackwood, Andrew W., Jr., *The Voice from the Cross: Sermons on the Seven Words from the Cross.* Grand Rapids: Baker Book House, 1965.

Boice, James M. *The Christ of the Empty Tomb.* Chicago: Moody Press, 1985.

Clow, W. M. *The Day of the Cross: A Course of Sermons on the Men and Women and Some of the Notable Things of the Day of the Crucifixion of Jesus.* 1909. Reprint. Grand Rapids: Baker Book House, 1955.

Great Sermons on the Resurrection by Alexander Maclaren, C. H. Spurgeon, D. L. Moody, T. DeWitt Talmadge, and Canon Liddon. Grand Rapids: Baker Book House, 1963.

Hageman, Howard G. *We Call This Friday Good.* Philadelphia: Fortress Press, 1961.

Holt, John A. *Dialogue at Calvary or The Seven Words to the Cross.* Grand Rapids: Baker Book House, 1965.

Jones, Russell Bradley. *Gold From Golgotha.* Chicago: Moody Press, 1945.

King, Geoffrey R. *The Forty Days.* 4th ed. London: Henry E. Walter, 1983.

Krummacher, F. W. *The Suffering Savior.* Chicago: Moody Press, 1947.

Loane, Marcus L. *The Place Called Calvary.* Grand Rapids: Zondervan Publishing House.

Long, S. P. *The Wounded Word: A Brief Meditation on the Seven Sayings of Christ on the Cross.* Grand Rapids: Baker Book House, 1966.

Maclaren, Alexander, and Henry Barclay Swete. *The Post-Resurrection Ministry of Christ.* 2 vols. in 1. Minneapolis: Klock and Klock Christian Publishers, 1985.

McDowell, Josh. *The Resurrection Factor*. San Bernardino, Calif.: Here's Life Publishers, 1982.

Morison, Frank [pseud.]. *Who Moved the Stone?* New ed. London: Faber and Faber, 1958.

Orr, James. *The Resurrection of Jesus*. Grand Rapids: Zondervan Publishing House, 1965.

Pink, Arthur W. *The Seven Sayings of the Saviour on the Cross*. Grand Rapids: Baker Book House, 1958.

Simpson, Hubert. *Testament of Love*. New York: Abingdon, 1935.

Simpson, William John Sparrow. *Our Lord's Resurrection*. Grand Rapids: Zondervan Publishing House, 1964.

―――. *The Resurrection and the Christian Faith*. Grand Rapids: Zondervan Publishing House, 1968.

Spurgeon, Charles Haddon. *Christ's Words from the Cross*. Grand Rapids: Zondervan Publishing House, 1965.

Stalker, James. *The Trials and Death of Jesus Christ: A Devotional History of our Lord's Passion*. London: Hodder & Stoughton, 1894.

Stott, John R. W. *The Cross of Christ*. Downer's Grove, Ill.: InterVarsity Press, 1986.

Tatham, C. Ernest. *He Lives*. Chicago: Moody Press, 1963.

Tenney, Merrill C. *The Reality of the Resurrection*. New York: Harper & Row, 1963.

Wallace, Ronald S. *Words of Triumph: The Words from the Cross and Their Application Today*. Richmond, Va.: John Knox Press, 1964.

Part 2: Christmas

Criswell, W. A., *Isaiah: An Exposition*. Grand Rapids: Zondervan Publishing House, 1977.

Delitzsch, Franz. *Commentary on Isaiah*. 2 vols. Reprint. Grand Rapids: Wm. B. Eerdmans Publishing Co., 1949.

Henstenberg, Ernst Wilhelm. *Christology of the Old Testament*. 4 vols. Grand Rapids: Kregel Publications, 1956.

Ironside, H. A. *Expository Notes on the Prophet Isaiah*. New York: Loizeaux Brothers, Inc., 1952.

Jennings, F. C. *Studies in Isaiah*. Neptune, N.J.: Loizeaux Brothers, Inc., 1966.

Meyer, F. B. *Christ in Isaiah*. 1895. Reprint. Fort Washington, Pa.: Christian Literature Crusade, 1970.

Wiersbe, W. W. *His Name Is Wonderful*. Wheaton, Ill.: Tyndale, 1976.